LEX SCHOLASTICUS JOURNAL OF SOCIO-ECONOMIC ISSUES (VOLUME II - ISSUE I)

LEX SCHOLASTICUS

Made with ♥ on the Notion Press Platform
www.notionpress.com

Contents

CHAPTER I

The economic downfall of India in contrast with gender understanding

Written by Kushagra Saxena (Data Scientist & Political Commentator).

Abstract

This paper examines the macroeconomic interaction between informality and gender inequality in the labor market. A dynamic stochastic general equilibrium model is built to study the impact of gender-targeted policies on female labor force participation, formal female employment, gender wage gap, as well as on aggregate economic outcomes. The model is estimated using Bayesian techniques and Indian data. Although these policies are found to increase female labor force participation and output, lack of sufficient formal job creation due to labor market rigidities leads to an increase in unemployment and informality, and further widens gender gaps in formal employment and wages. Simultaneously implementing such policies with formal job-creating policies helps remove these adverse impacts while also leading to significantly larger gains in output.

Keywords: gender inequality, informality, DSGE model, Indian economy

Introduction

Gender inequality is one of the biggest challenges facing Indian policy makers trying to achieve faster, sustainable, and more inclusive growth. In particular, division along gender lines in the labor market is one of the key concerns. For instance, India's female labor force participation rate is the third lowest in the South Asian region at 27 percent in 2011-12; and less than one-third of male labor participation of 84 percent. In addition, they receive lower wages, are overrepresented in informal and unpaid domestic work, with gender gaps existing along several other dimensions including education, access to productive inputs, and bargaining power at home

Notwithstanding rising education levels amongst women in India, female labor participation has been declining and fell from 34 percent in 1999-00 to 27 percent in 2011-12, in both rural and urban areas. Lack of decent quality jobs in the formal economy discourage female participation. More than 80 percent of the workforce is employed informally in India, and among the ones that are employed in the formal sector, females constitute only 19-20 percent (Consensus 2011). Rigidities in the labor market due to strict regulations have been identified as the main drivers of this large informality.

Literature Survey

Now we turn to comparing our work with the existing theoretical policy literature on gender inequality. A considerably vast literature has investigated the effects of gender-specific policies in competitive labour markets. Female labour supply in these models is often modeled using the framework of the time allocation model, where women's labour supply decision is based not only on the trade-off between leisure and labour, but also on home production modeled as investment in childcare. These studies analyze the impact of one or more of the following policies: increase in female education, increase in childcare provisions, better access to infrastructure, as well as fall in exogenously given gender wage discrimination. In sum, their results suggest that each of the above policies increase female labour participation that has a positive impact on their productivity, hence leading to higher growth. One or more of the following channels drive these results: (i) higher female labour participation increases female employment (under the assumption of flexible labour markets) and females' labour income; (ii) this increase in females' income improves the average human capital (skill) in the economy, as females are assumed to invest more in children's education relative to males; and (iii) higher participation, in turn, has a direct effect on per capita GDP, as females move from unpaid home-good production (not accounted for in GDP) into market-good production.

Why is the gap widening?

The gap is widening mainly due to India's global rank when it comes to political empowerment among women. India ranks 48th in the world currently. This may appear like a good thing, but in 2016, the country was the ninth in the world. The rank then fell to 15 in 2017, 19 in 2018 and then to 51 in 2021. "Political Empowerment records a declining score (in India) due to the diminishing share of years women have served as head of state for the past 50 years," the latest report says.

Which are the parameters in which the country fared badly?

India has the lowest ranks in Health and Survival, and Economic Participation and Opportunity. In both parameters, the country has scored 143rd rank among 146 countries. India's score and ranking in these parameters have always been low. The rank in the former has been low, owing to low sex ratio at birth, according to the report. According to the latest National Family Health Survey (NFHS), sex ratio at birth for children born in the last five years was 929 females per 1,000 males. However, the World Health Organisation (WHO) has estimated that the natural sex ratio at birth is about 952 females to every 1,000 males.

When it comes to Economic Participation and Opportunity, the Periodic Labour Force Survey's 2020-21 annual report says that labour force participation rate among Indian women is just 23.15 per cent, in contrast to 57.75 per cent in men. According to NFHS 2019-21, 25.2 per cent of the women surveyed were employed, while 74.8 per cent of the surveyed men had a job at that point.

"The most unequal economies with less than 65 per cent of wealth equity are Nigeria, Argentina, Mexico, Turkey and India," the Gender Gap Report says. This means, in these countries women accumulate less than 65 per cent of the wealth men create at retirement, on average. India's score here is between 60 and 64 per cent.

What needs to be done to arrest this decline?

The report criticises the rising inequality in the number of women holding offices in India. Passing the Women's Reservation Bill that proposes to reserve 33 per cent of all seats in the Lok Sabha and in all State legislative assemblies for women could make this situation better. Measures could also be taken to address the gender wage gap across industries. According to the estimates of the World Inequality Report 2022, in India, men earn 82 per cent of the labour income whereas women earn 18 per cent of it. Also, there is scope to allocate more money towards the gender budget, which aims to ensure that women have access to socio-economic benefits as much as men.

Conclusion

In this paper, we investigate the interaction between informality and gender inequality in the labor market. Specifically, we study the impact of a number of gender-specific policies on female labor force participation, their access to formal employment, gender wage gaps, as well as on aggregate economic outcomes.

CHAPTER II

Analysing the imperialism of existing Kingdoms and the reason for their survival.

Written by Prishita Vatsayan (2nd Semester, BA. LL.B - Chandigarh University, Mohali).

Abstract

Imperialism is the state's strategy, practice, or promotion of expanding its realm of influence, particularly through the direct conquest of new territories or through the establishment of political and economic dominance over other peoples and nations. Imperialism has frequently been viewed as immoral because it always entails the use of force, whether military, economic, or in some other subtle way. One of the earliest sorts of societies on Earth, kingdoms have existed for thousands of years. Kingdoms, like the United Kingdom, can be enormous. The United Kingdom, which was governed from London, England, throughout the nineteenth century, included five continents. The kingdom of Brunei, which is smaller than the state of Delaware in the United States, is an example of a tiny kingdom. Rarely is an absolute monarch, a single king or queen who rules over the whole state, in charge of a kingdom. Kingdoms are frequently divided into smaller areas, such as city-states or provinces, which are run by administrators who answer to the king or queen. Most kings and queens in contemporary times do not rule over the country. Most kingdoms nowadays have constitutions and elected kings who set the laws. A time in history known as the Middle Ages spanned around 500 to 1500.

Keywords: Imperialism, Capitalist, Kingdom, Socialist, Monarch & Capitalist.

Introduction

Imperialism is a global hierarchy in which one political community subjugates or essentially rules over another political society. It can also be defined as any escalation in authority or power or support for such escalation. Imperialism is a domination and power dynamic, consequently, it is unable to exist without at least the threat of violence. For instance, blatant violence, such as war and so-called "punitive expeditions," was a major component of colonial administration over indigenous communities. Economic imperialism insists that the fundamental standard for determining success and failure in every area be money and material ownership, therefore, be regarded more than anything else as a result. Imperialism was not always primarily a matter of metropolitan governments. People of different social groups and professions acted as protagonists of expansion.

As a matter of fact, in established colonies, state leaders like viceroys and governors frequently had a strong interest in future expansion since it would help them advance professionally and boost their reputation. In order to support the emergence of colony-to-colony circuits of knowledge and technology transfer, imperialism relied on international circuits of knowledge and technology transfer that transported knowledge from the metropolitan centre to the colonial peripheries, as a result, new hybridised architectural typologies and styles emerged. Imperial metropolitan cities' architecture frequently adopted forms and symbols from local architectural customs in their territories. The strongly modernist ideals embraced in post-independence city development projects like those in Chandigarh and Brasilia are evidence of this tendency. The modernist aesthetic used in such plans provided a formal clarity that drastically altered and even shed the past.

Existing Kingdom

Royal families exist in nations with monarchies, and historically, a monarch's family would consist of their spouse, children, and grandchildren, as well as any surviving parents, siblings, and paternal relatives. Out of the 26 monarchs in the globe, 12 are found in Europe, and a royal family is in charge of 10 of them. This includes well-known royal families like the Windsors in the United Kingdom and the Grimaldis in Monaco. The Windsor family, possibly the most well-known royal family worldwide, is the reigning dynasty of much more than simply the United Kingdom, a little-known truth in many nations. Monarchies are typically connected with the hereditary rule in political and sociocultural studies; most monarchs, in both historical and modern contexts, were born and nurtured in royal families.

Many other equations, including closeness of blood, primogeniture, and agnatic seniority, have been used to define succession. 43 independent states will exist on the planet as of 2022, with 13 in Asia, 12 in Europe, 9 in the Americas, 6 in Oceania, and 3 in Africa. Various monarchies include in addition to being constitutional monarchies and complete democracies, King Charles III is the ruler of fifteen Commonwealth states. They separated themselves from the British Empire and became completely independent states within the Commonwealth of Nations, keeping the same King as their head of state. Other European constitutional monarchies, including those in Belgium, Denmark, Norway, Spain, and Sweden, are fully democratic nations where the monarch generally serves as a figurehead. In a European hybrid monarchy, the Prince retains many of the powers of an absolute monarch, for instance, the Prince of Monaco can appoint judges, governing council members, and ministers of state. Then there are non-sovereign monarchies, in which both the king and the monarchical polity are subordinate to a sovereign state such as the Emirates of the United Arab Emirates and the Kingdoms of Uganda.

The Existing Kingdoms include, for example, The Vatican City State which is ruled by an elected absolute theocracy, the Pope is the Head of State and during a papal conclave, the College of Cardinals elects the Pope. The President of the Governorate of Vatican City State, who the Pope chooses for a five-year term, serves as the head of the government of Vatican City. Pope Francis, who holds total authority in the tiny autonomous city of the Vatican, is another exceptional occurrence. He was elected to his position through a procedure known as a papal conclave. The Vatican City is different from the Holy See despite being closely related to it. Foreign embassies are accredited to the Holy See, which also makes treaties and concordats controlling relations between the Papacy and other institutions.

The Holy See, not the Vatican City, maintains diplomatic relations with other sovereign governments, some of the previous treaty clauses, particularly the supremacy of Roman Catholicism as the Italian state religion, were changed by a concordat between the Holy See and Italy in 1984. The Roman Catholic Church's administrative centre is located in the State of Vatican City. The VHS's ongoing interchange of representatives with states has a missionary, hierarchical character, and it does not reflect the duty of peers to one another or the legal force of custom. The 1929 Lateran Pacts, which the papacy and the Kingdom of Italy signed over the status of the area known as Vatican City, cannot be used to determine a country's standing internationally. Additionally, participation in international accords and organisations does not grant a status equivalent to statehood. The international status as of 1870 has not significantly changed as a result of events and behaviours since 1929. The Roman Catholic Church is only one of several global movements that are founded on religion. Events and actions after 1929 have not appreciably altered the international position as of 1870. One of the international movements with religious roots is the Roman Catholic Church.

King Charles is now the king and head of state of the UK and 14 other nations, collectively referred to as Commonwealth realms, as a result of British colonialism, which saw the British Empire attack and conquers territories all over the world for centuries. The Commonwealth realms include Antigua and Barbuda, Australia, The Bahamas, Belize, Canada, Grenada, Jamaica, New Zealand, Papua New Guinea, Saint Kitts and Nevis, Saint Lucia, Saint Vincent and the Grenadines, Solomon Islands, and Tuvalu. Even while the Commonwealth kingdoms represent evidence of the British Empire's continuing heritage, they also remind us that, throughout Queen Elizabeth's reign, the empire was in decline. During her reign, she served as the leader of 32 nations, however, 17 of those nations ended their relations with her at the same time. Sri Lanka, Fiji, The Gambia, Ghana, Guyana, Kenya, Malawi, Malta, Mauritius, Nigeria, Pakistan, Sierra Leone, South Africa, Tanzania (Tanganyika), Trinidad and Tobago, and Uganda are among the 16 nations that deposed Queen Elizabeth as head of state when she gained the throne in 1952.

Charles also becomes prime minister during a precarious period for British politics, when the nation is dealing with the worst inflation since the 1970s and skyrocketing oil prices.

"The Crown is an integral part of the institution of Parliament. The Queen [now King] plays a constitutional role in opening and dissolving Parliament and approving Bills before they become law". -BRITISH PARLIAMENT.

Can Monarchs be directly proportiona to Socialists?

In his Arthashastra, Kautilya proposed a system of government-based economics. He argued that a king's responsibility is to ensure the well-being of his subjects to the greatest extent possible and that if he fails in this, the subjects have the right to reject the monarch as their ruler. To promote the welfare of the subjects, he encouraged the monarch to implement a mixed economy with considerable control over every sector of the economy. Consequently, this was the earliest instance of a socialist economy of the sort found in Yugoslavia in the prehistoric era.

For example, the story of King Vikramaditya depicts the ideal monarch as being more socialist than monarchical. Before 1068, Vikramaditya demonstrated his military aspirations while still a prince. According to legend, Akbar, Krishnadev Rai, and Vikramaditya all borrowed the practice of gathering nine luminaries in the court from Vikramaditya's court. The stories of Vikramaditya's statecraft and polity are full of lessons that many modern-day leaders and administrative officials might benefit from. As the prince of Ujjain, Vikramaditya was born to king Gandharvasena. At the young age of five, he began to lead an austere life, and after twelve years of meditation, he ascended to the throne. An educated Brahmin interrupted the ceremony as he was ready to assume the throne decorated with 32 golden statues to instruct him on the duties of a king and the art of statecraft. He took the kingdom and drove the Shakas out, travelling as far as Bactria, after gaining the instruction necessary for an effective monarch.

Chandragupta II, who reigned from 375 AD to 414 AD, was chosen especially by his father because of his aptitude and competency. Chandragupta II led the conquest of the globe, much like his father. The king was at the apex of the administration. As the head of the state has the embodiment of the mighty and majesty of the nation. He served as the administration's unifying source of law. Kautilya asserts that the four pillars of law are deharina, contract, custom, and regal decorum. This indicates that the king's order or decorum was supreme to all other laws. The monarch, therefore, governed in accordance with the law, customs, and the council of Ministers' recommendations. The village tribunals were at the bottom of a series of courts. Smaller local conflicts are often resolved by the village headman and elders. Higher courts came in the civil and criminal varieties. The "Dharamasthaniya" Courts were the name of the civil courts. Three Amatyas, with the assistance of three Dharmastha, were in charge of the civil courts. Court cases involving disagreements over marriage, divorce, dowries, property inheritance, homes, lands, borders, debts, contracts, and other issues were heard there.

Three Amatyas presided over the criminal tribunals known as the "Kantarodhna" Courts with the help of many spies and aqeuts. Murderers, national traitors, political offenders, thieves, lawbreakers, and criminals were all prosecuted in such tribunals. This military organisation was incredibly sophisticated and effective. The Senapati, the highest-ranking officer in the army, earned a pay equivalent to that of the High Minister. 60,000 soldiers, 60,000 horsemen, 3,000 chariots, and 9,000 elephants made comprised Chandragupta Maurya's large and effective army, according to Megasthenes. A thirty-member council that was further split into six Boards of five men each effectively organised the army.

In particular, the first board collaborated with the admiral and was in command of the Navy. The state looked after the ships. The second board, which was in charge of supplies and transportation, collaborated with the bullock-cart superintendent. The third board was in command of the Pahvadhayaksha's soldiers. The warriors had swords, javelins, and bows and arrows at their disposal. In control of the cavalry was the fourth board. In command of the war, the elephant was the fifth board. The war chariots are overseen by the Sixth Board. And finally, during the reign of the Mauryas, the spy system significantly aided the government and the monarch in carrying out their duties. They also provided information to the relatives and stayed abreast with popular sentiment on significant issues. The province was split into several Janapadas ordinaries each Janapadas into some Gangs or sthanas and each sthana into some villages for administrative convenience. The region was administered by the Sthanikas and Gopas. The Gopa controlled five to ten villages, but the Sthanika was in command of one larger area or Janapada. The Minister of Finance and the Interior, Sameharta, was in charge of the Sthanikas and Gopas. The village served as the lowest level of government. With the assistance of local elders, the gramik, or village headman, oversaw each village's administration. Villages delighted in autonomy. His successors continued his empire's administrations in the same manner since no changes were deemed essential, demonstrating that he was not just a great conqueror but also an effective administrator.

Can Capitalists and Monarchs be compared directly?

Economics of the form of capitalism. One sort of governance is the monarchy. Monarchy is comparable to fully perfected capitalism. A privately held kingdom may function similarly since privately owned capital is more effective and productive. The economic expression of democracy is capitalism, which is also a contributing factor to the institution of monarchy's decline and corruption. The optimal economic system for a monarchy, in my opinion, would be very dependent on its economic goals, its location in terms of both geography and politics, the concentration of its resources, etc. the elite planners of the governing class. Johnson has used the Queen to draw attention to the Monarchy's true powers—powers that, in the eyes of the establishment, are best kept concealed in the background. The serious strategists of the ruling class, for instance in the UK. Johnson has used the Queen to draw attention to the Monarchy's true powers—powers that, in the eyes of the establishment, are best kept concealed in the background. The Tory cabinet is therefore tried to bring back Buckingham Palace into a full-fledged constitutional crisis by including the Queen in pushing through a no-deal Brexit. There could already be too many scandals for the monarchy.

The monarchy is really maintained as a standby weapon for the ruling elite. The function of the monarchy in times of crisis has come to light thanks to the most recent constitutional issue in Britain. The ruling class took action to strengthen the monarchical institution at the conclusion of Queen Victoria's reign and the start of the 20th century by lavishly spending massive quantities of money on grand spectacles like Victoria's Golden Jubilee in 1887. The majority of today's ceremonial pantomimes, which most people mistakenly believe to be ages-old British customs, were created during this period. The expansion of the vote and universal male suffrage kept the monarchy in power. According to The Economist magazine, the governing class thought the country needed the monarchy as a symbol of stability and they needed it to assist them in keeping control of the government after being obliged to expand the voting franchise. Britain lacks a written constitution, unlike other nations. The majority of laws are derived from custom and usage. But precisely because of this, there are lots of ambiguities.

What would happen, for instance, if an elected government tried to seize control of the banks and monopolies? Bagehot responds with his characteristic candour. The illiterate people don't comprehend politics and can't truly be trusted with the vote, wrote Walter Bagehot in one of his writings, The English Constitution. However, now that they have gained the right to vote, the ruling class must create some sort of charade to appease them while maintaining strict control over the actual exercise of power. In order to draw attention away from the reality of the situation, it is worth investing some actual money in ceremony and glitter. It is crucial that the general populace respects the monarchy. Therefore, this investment is valuable, just like any other.

In the event that something goes wrong horribly, it is also required insurance coverage. The Blairites' support of the monarchy is the most egregious illustration of how the right-wing modernizers have abandoned even the most basic socialist ideals. Even those who advocate for its removal lack comprehension of the monarchy's issues; they believe it to be nothing more than a costly anachronism. It is hard to determine the Queen's true fortune. The Queen is a member of the capitalist class with an investment portfolio that is conservatively valued at over £250 million. She is said to stand above classes and party politics. The millions thrown out on this group of parasitic idlers might and ought to be used to fund institutions like homes, hospitals, and schools. The ruling elite will want to keep the monarchy in place as a defence against the labour movement and a barrier to social advancement.

Monarchy is incomplete without an ambition of Imperilism

The monarchy is still in existence partly because it is an imperialist relic, pomp and circumstance-filled anachronism that receives feverish and voluminous coverage from the media. It is a business tool that has reached the end of its useful life and should be retired. The implementation of the Treaty of Versailles and the upholding of the Peace enter a new chapter with the start of the London Conference. France had wholeheartedly contributed to the implementation of Edward VII's agenda. France might easily and at the appropriate time be drawn into a conflict with Germany by the retaliatory attitude that still lurks under the surface. That is what took place in 1914. It provided the majority of the casualties, and its region served as the battleground. Great Britain and France were in quite different places once the fighting was over. The war objectives of the former were met. Only its remnants remained for the latter. Great Britain and France were in quite different places once the fighting was over. The war objectives of the former were met. Only its remnants remained for the latter.

The new states that have emerged from the battle and are gathered must be ruled by the policy. It supplied them with military instructors and ammunition, as well as to Poland. With Poincaré's help, France decided to occupy the

Ruhr in order to solidify that occupation and, at the same time, fulfil the goals of the Comité des Forges. The goal of French imperialism is being approached. Its finances at the time were the major issue. In actuality, the French State was insolvent. British imperialism, concerned about French predominance in Europe, launched its offensive at this vulnerable spot. A magnificent onslaught is launched against the franc, whose demise appears to be disastrous. Poincaré must make a plea to the American and English financiers and agree to their demands in order to avoid falling. He had previously criticised international money as an arcane and wicked force, but now he is forced to commit himself to accept its conditions because of threats. Before he fell, Hitler agreed "without conditions or reservations" to the experts' proposal, which calls for the evacuation of the Ruhr.

Modern Imperilism

The continued presence of colonialism is not refuted by contemporary imperialism. Natural resource theft, military occupation, direct governmental control over colonies, and the theft of goods not created through capitalism by imperialist nations are all examples of colonialism. By exchanging commodities with high technological content produced in the imperialist countries for raw materials or industrial goods produced with lower technological content in the dominated countries, colonialism refers to the appropriation of the surplus value produced by capitals in the colonies by capitals in the imperialist countries. Unfair exchange and the expropriation of global excess value through trade are the outcomes. In colonialism, this contemporary method of appropriating global surplus wealth was present. Colonialism is penetrated by modern imperialism and grows inside it until it takes the lead.

In the global economy and, to a lesser extent, as the world's top military force, China has emerged as the main rival to the United States, a system of international competition that forces the Chinese government to act imperialistically in order to advance the interests of Chinese capital. The leaders of China continue to use state power to further their own interests in opposition to those of other powerful nations. State capitalists in charge of China have the same interests as the ruling elite in the US. China is becoming a significant global force, able to advance and protect its economic and military interests across Asia and beyond. When China ratified Western economic standards when it joined the World Trade Organization (WTO) in December 2001. Greater chances for Western capital were promised by China's post-Mao economic liberalisation.

By utilising the 200 million rural migrants who have entered China's major industrial cities since the early 1990s, these capitals planned to address the profitability dilemma that had plagued them since the 1970s. Three decades of US-China rivalry that periodically threatened armed confrontation were followed by WTO membership. China has transitioned from being a strategic ally to a worldwide competition, according to US strategists. With the West, it is entangled in an inter-imperialist competition. China became the second-largest power in the world at the start of the twenty-first century, in the centre of capitalist globalisation. The Chinese state, which controls the China aircraft and can enforce its rules in important economic sectors, feeds a massive patronage system bolstered by the party's power to impose pervasive social monitoring.

In Asia, the nation driving economic progress is nothing new, from India to South Korea. The socioeconomic structure of China is extremely diverse, and as a global manufacturing hub, its economy depends in part on the importation of raw materials and replacement parts. It does, however, provide the framework for autonomous global growth. The dominant branch of the global bourgeoisie committed the error of triumphalism, believing that its undivided dominance was now secured in the wake of the 1980s international defeat of the revolutionary movements and the collapse of the USSR. It appears that it was unaware that Beijing could successfully employ the neoliberal international order it created to its benefit. Imperialism is a trait shared by all major capitalist powers. Several instances are while securing access to the Indian Ocean and safeguarding its investments in the age of the new Silk Roads while securing a permit to the Indian Ocean and safeguarding its investments in the age of the new Silk Roads, China is now participating in the delineation of South Pacific Ocean zones of influence by claiming a sizable maritime region as part of its international self-projection. In response to the US threat, the Maoist dictatorship devised a defensive strategy, the army, public mobilisation, and the size of the nation serving as its pillars: an invader would get lost there.

Uprising against maintance of Monarchs and Capitalists

A less extreme version of anti-royalism that has been successful in some countries that still have monarchs is the abolition of absolutist monarchy in favour of restricted rule under a constitutional monarchy. Nearly no one could conceive France being ruled without a king, despite the monarchy's constant battle with elites over the meaning of royal power. Only a small percentage of the populace had ever considered a republic at the commencement of the Revolution. The convocation of the Estates-General was welcomed by French people from all socioeconomic classes, but there was considerable debate about how it should be chosen and run its proceedings. The clergy, aristocracy, and commons were the three estates that made up the Estates-General in the past, and each had an equal number of representatives. Each estate only had one vote. Since the bulk of the clergy representatives were nobles, the nobility always had sway in this system. Leading nobility wanted to keep the custom of vote by order, as it would have guaranteed their control. Leading Third Estate deputies came to the conclusion within a month that if they wanted to share in the power, they would have to take it. The Third Estate representatives asserted that only they had the authority to form the body exercising true political sovereignty since they alone represented the country.

The King hesitated to acknowledge the Third Estate representatives as the National Assembly because he was unsure of how to react to this assertion of national sovereignty. At the same time, Louis consented to adopt the constitutional monarchy, which would allow him to rule alongside rather than above his subjects. The King was consistently and truly popular throughout this time and he represented France's greatest chance of finding a solution. The King and Queen's overall issues were most obvious in October 1789. Bread costs in the nation's capital continued to be among the highest of the century despite the persistent political conflict between the King and the National Assembly. Women gathered at the Parisian market to demonstrate. They were accompanied by other National Guard troops as they headed to Versailles to file their complaints. The crowd effectively kidnapped the royal family when they arrived at the royal palace in the middle of the night and forced them to leave for Paris in order to pressure the King into taking action to lower bread prices and keep the Revolution going. Despite the King's triumphant return to Paris, widespread protests were evident.

The Civil Constitution of the Clergy, which restructured the Catholic Church in France, was the issue that led the King to rebel against the new government. The National Assembly enacted legislation making the clergy electable, and those who were chosen signed an oath of allegiance to the new government. This action dealt a blow to the ecclesiastical establishment by eliminating the royal and papal authority over clergy appointments. Some members of the King's entourage had been pleading with him to leave the nation since 1789 so he wouldn't have to give up his ostensibly unchallengeable authority. He accepted a plan to escape in secret rather than approve the new constitution, which sparked a military invasion by antirevolutionary nobility with help from the Habsburg Emperor Leopold II. Later in June, the royal family travelled to the border while posing as servants. The royal family left towards the border while posing as servants.

The Cuban Revolution was the most significant socialist/communist revolution in the Americas in the 1900s. Led by Fidel Castro (1926–2016) and Che Guevara (1928–1967), the participants overthrew Cuba's capitalist system, which had become beholden to U.S. commercial interests. They replaced it with a communist system that is still in place today. The philosophies of capitalism and communism were always at odds with one another between the United States and the Soviet Union. Cuba has been in a state of near civil conflict since Castro's arrival. In a brutal and ultimately fruitless assault on the Havana presidential palace, the Revolutionary Directorate, a group of insurrectionists primarily made up of students, started their uprising and there are reports of dozens of deaths during the conflict. The government's announcement that anyone engaging in the strike would be prohibited from finding new job elsewhere caused labour leaders to abandon their support for the trade unionists' attempts to incite a nationwide strike.

In 1958, the revolution continued with irregular attacks and significant property damage as the turmoil started to substantially impair the Cuban economy. Burning of sugar mills and farms, bombings in Havana that hurt tourism, and insurgent action in the Oriente area that hurt mining. The presidential elections were postponed as a result of the United States' mid-March imposition of an arms embargo on Cuba. Castro, for his part, made a variety of proclamations throughout the year, ranging from calls for a national strike to threats to kill all political candidates. The abduction of 10 Americans and 2 Canadians from the Freeport Sulphur company's mining offices in northeastern Cuba was one of Castro's many adventures. The next day, 28 American servicemen were abducted from a bus outside the military facility at Guantánamo Bay. Castro threatened violence against candidates and voters in the days leading up to the election as the revised election date drew near. There were three major contenders. But when the election results were made public, it was obvious that there had been a significant amount of fraud. The history of the Cuban Revolution may have been extremely different if Márquez Sterling had won the election. Guevara was to get the designation of native-born Cuban under the new system, making him eligible for any government job, including the presidency.

In the months that followed, Che Guevara would preside over military jails, preside over courts martial, and travel widely throughout Asia, North Africa, and the Soviet Union. Triumphant trips to neighbouring nations defined the early stages of his presidency, and at a speech in Caracas, Venezuela, he declared that the proletarian revolution was taking place in the Americas. When questioned about the veracity of the quotation, Castro subtly disingenuously said that Cuba was impoverished and lacked both troops and weapons but had yet been quoted as having indicated that Cuba would remain neutral in any conflict between the West and the Soviet bloc. Castro swiftly moved to expropriation, forced loans, additional and higher taxes, and exchange control when his goodwill mission failed to extract any financial assistance from the United States. Because Castro's position was far from secure during his first year in office, the consolidation of power was required.

The economy of Cuba was in ruins, with unemployment skyrocketing and private investment falling. Falling prices for sugar, tobacco, and other essentials on the Cuban export market made the situation worse. However, by October 1959, both the central and western regions of Cuba were experiencing actual upheavals. These early attempts to overthrow Castro were unsuccessful. The signing of a commercial agreement with the Soviet Union in February 1960 marked a strengthening of Cuba's ties to Moscow. Castro then proceeded to the United Nations, where he openly welcomed Soviet leader Nikita Khrushchev and gave a four-and-a-half-hour address criticising the United States. Despite protestations from the United States, the expropriation of foreign assets persisted, and by the end of 1960, little economic exchange still took place between the United States and Cuba. President Dwight D. Eisenhower of the United States cut off diplomatic ties with Cuba in 1961, one of his final acts in office. 1961 saw the severing of diplomatic ties with Cuba, one of Dwight D. Eisenhower's final acts as president of the United States. At the Bay of Pigs, some 1,500 Cuban exiles who had been supported and led by the American Central Intelligence Agency mounted an unsuccessful invasion. The last significant overt effort to remove the Castro dictatorship was the invasion, which was thwarted by the Cuban military.

Conclusion

In this article, we learned the fundamentals of imperialism and how it relates to capitalism and socialism. Somewhere globalization was a result of imperialism; by expanding abroad, each country's prosperity was increased. Compared to an unofficial empire, colonisation had a greater negative effect. Metropolitan nations exploited colonies for their own gain and seldom enjoyed economic progress, whereas nations governed by the informal sector did so but without successfully diversifying their economy. Following Schumpeter's conclusion—that contemporary imperialism is not a byproduct of capitalism—is the dominant tendency in academic thought in the Western world. The New Imperialism put an end to the uncertainty surrounding the selection of imperialist military and political strategies.

References

- https://www.sciencedirect.com/topics/socialsciences/imperialism#:~:text=Imperialism%20is%20a%20form%20of,and%20Rome%20through%20modern%20Europe.
- https://www.infoplease.com/world/social-statistics/kingdoms-and-monarchs-world
- https://in.docworkspace.com/d/sANlUppuFu6K2AZXbu6CvpxQ
- https://www.thenation.com/article/world/king-charles-windsor-monarchy-class/
- https://www.washingtonpost.com/world/2022/09/14/uk-king-charles-win-monarchy-support/
- https://www.businessinsider.in/politics/world/news/due-to-british-colonialism-king-charles-is-now-the-monarch-of-14-countries-in-addition-to-the-uk-following-queen-elizabeths-death/articleshow/94084900.cms

- https://www.nationsonline.org/oneworld/vatican.htm#:~:text=It%20is%20the%20world's%20smallest,the%20Holy%20See%20and%20Italy.
- https://www.visualcapitalist.com/which-countries-still-have-monarchy/

CHAPTER III

China's Zero Covid Policy

Written by Ashay Kumar Yadav (8th Semester, BA. LL.B - Chandigarh University, Mohali) & Shirish Birendra Singh (8th Semester, BA. LL.B - Chandigarh University, Mohali).

Introduction

China's strict pandemic restrictions have sparked protests all over the country. The demonstrations suggest that China's "zero-COVID" policy's prolonged lockdowns and widespread testing have worn out many Chinese. In the fight against COVID-19, China wants to keep the number of cases as low as possible. It has carried out extensive testing, quarantined the ill in government facilities, and imposed strict lockdowns that can span entire cities in order to accomplish this. China astounded the world when it secured the whole city of Wuhan during the underlying episode of the infection in 2019, limiting in excess of 11 million occupants to their homes. China has since adopted the same strategies as part of its zero-COVID strategy. As per statistics,

Doses of COVID vaccine as compared to April 2022 to November 2022 are

- First Dose: April 2022- 58.8% November 2022 - 76.6%
- Second Dose: April 2022- 50.7% November 2022 - 65.8 %
- Booster Dose : April 2022- 19.7% November 2022 - 40.4%

When compared to Western nations, China claims that its strategy has kept coronavirus cases and deaths low. The Johns Hopkins Coronavirus Resource Center reports that of China's 1.4 billion people, nearly 16,000 have died from COVID-19, while the United States, which has been hardest hit by the pandemic, has reported more than a million deaths.

What is zero Covid policy according to China?

Even if only a small number of cases are reported, this policy in China orders cities to enforce strict lockdowns and social isolation measures. The strategy aims to prevent new infection and eradicate the virus so that the country can resume normal social and economic activities. The 26 million people who live in Shanghai had to follow the most stringent procedures as the number of cases increased. Extreme measures were being taken to eradicate the virus, including isolating individuals and separating families when a person tested positive. The public is experiencing emotional turmoil as a result of these measures because, after separation, essential medical treatments are delayed due to administrative issues, extending the separation period.

Additionally, incidents have been reported in which individuals who tested negative were taken to quarantine facilities and forced to grant access to their residence in order to disinfect it. People are feeling resentment toward the government's oppressiveness.ii The public is pleading for assistance in videos that are being shared on social media platforms for a variety of reasons, including the lack of food, the delay in receiving treatment, the separation of infants from their parents, and other issues. China's authorities, on the other hand, have reiterated that the policy is necessary to save lives and denied all allegations. At first, it was thought that China was handling the virus fairly well. However, Dr. Tedros Adhanom Ghebreyesu of the World Health Organization (WHO) recently emphasized that since the virus is changing, it is important to implement new measures as well. The zero-Covid policy fails to achieve its goal because new coronavirus variants are becoming more transmissible; recent outbreaks of Delta and Omicron variants in various Chinese cities demonstrate this.

China's Economy

The Chinese economy is once again experiencing the negative effects of Covid-19 as a result of the authorities' stringent mitigation strategy, despite a sharp economic recovery following the first wave in 2020. China's commodity development declined to its most reduced since June 2020 in April and the imports were likewise stale for the month predominantly because of a muffled homegrown interest. The lockdown of factories in various cities as part of the zero COVID policy is primarily to blame for the decline in sector growth. Due to the stringent lockdowns that are disrupting the global supply chain, multinational corporations are also reporting decreased business confidence in China. iiiChina was able to control the virus with measures that involved isolating itself completely from the rest of the world and becoming selfreliant, and the domestic Chinese economy thrived initially under the zero COVID policy. The administration was able to control the virus's spread throughout the country because there was no perforated boundary.

However, despite recent outbreaks within the country, the government maintains a zero-covid policy, resulting in production and manufacturing being halted and lockdowns being imposed. The Chinese economy is suffering as a result of stringent restrictions on imports, exports, and people's movement within and outside the country.

The one area that Chinese policymakers do seem genuinely concerned about is real estate. China's real estate market is suffering, as house prices decline. What is more, homebuyers have threatened to stop paying mortgages on unfinished housing projects across the nation, leading to extreme cash flow problems among already-indebted property developers. This issue is important because it has resulted in social unrest, which Communist Party leaders are quick to quell to maintain social stability. To this end, Beijing has directed banks to bail out property developers. The aim here is not to promote economic reform and growth in this industry per se but to prevent social disruption.

Public response

Having endured the most stringent pandemic restrictions in the world for three years, thousands of Chinese have taken to the streets in numerous cities to demand an end to lockdowns and the "zero-COVID" policy. The decision Socialist Faction of China would do well to tune in. The public's dissatisfaction with a policy that seems out of date is reflected in the unprecedented protests on a scale not seen since 1989. China emerged faster than any other nation from the first COVID-19 wave than any other country, avoiding the mass deaths seen in the rest of the world thanks to the lockdowns, mass testing, and quarantining of infected cases, as well as close contacts. However, the emergence of milder, more transmissible variants has rendered this strategy increasingly obsolete, particularly as vaccines make it possible for countries to live with the virus. China has increased the severity of its lockdowns in response to new variants. Shanghai experienced a brutal two-month lockdown in March that resulted in a shortage of food and medicine.

It should not come as a surprise that China's largest city hosted one of the largest protests. As the social and economic costs of zero-COVID rise, the leadership will be concerned that the majority of young protesters' call to end lockdowns will resonate. Ten people were killed in a Urumqi apartment fire that sparked the protests. The lockdown measures were widely regarded as the reason for the slow emergency response.

Conclusion and Suggestions

Zero-COVID has been defended by the Chinese leadership, who have warned that opening up will result in mass deaths. However, this is only due to the fact that a significant portion of the elderly population is still unvaccinated. An urgent nationwide effort to vaccinate the vulnerable is long overdue rather than utilizing China's substantial state capacity to enforce lockdowns. Information from Hong Kong shows three dosages of Chinese antibodies, which are less successful than mRNA shots, do what is necessary safeguard the old. The issue is that China has been slow to vaccinate its people.iv Sixty-eight percent of the more than 250 million Chinese over the age of 60 had received three shots as of this month. Only 40% of the 30 million elderly Chinese have received three doses.

The public authority fears that opening up with such a huge weak populace would prompt a breakdown of China's medical services framework and harm its believability, with President Xi having by and by supported the zero-Coronavirus approach and outlined it as a differentiation toward the West, which has seen mass Coronavirus passings. It appears that the only way out is to complete vaccination coverage and simultaneously phase out the zero-COVID strategy.

A couple of conclusions can be drawn from China's COVID response. First, economic development is no longer the Communist Party's top priority. Over the past 30 years, Chinese officials could be counted on to place a high rate of growth before all other concerns. President Xi's stand on zero COVID despite its costs suggests that the party now favors political and social control over economic progress.

CHAPTER IV

Socio-economic Effects of Freebies and their Impact on the Indian Economy

Written by Arun Shekhar Jawla (8th Semester, BA. LL.B - Chandigarh University, Mohali).

Abstract

This paper will focus on the rising concern caused by the freebie culture. The discussion is mainly on how freebies burden the country's economy. Also, the difference between the welfare scheme and freebies will be explained in depth. Several primary resources include reports from the Reserve Bank of India (RBI), the Election Commission of India, and statistical data published by the Government of India are consulted for the article. Moreover, secondary sources, especially news articles, have also been utilized. The paper aims to make the readers aware of the economic pitfalls of freebies in the Indian economy by identifying markers that encourage such a culture. In addition, the paper makes a few remedial measures to battle the rising freebie culture.

Keywords: Freebie, Revadi Culture, Welfare Scheme, Debt, Economy, Free Electricity.

Introduction

Any interventions without medium to long-term positive impacts on future production and productivity are called freebies. Freebies are often talked about in the context of elections. Several free goods and services like electricity, water, education, buses, two-wheelers, kitchen appliances, and even gold are offered in the electoral campaigns. For instance, even gold has been used as a freebie in Tamil Naidu for women. This topic has become an essential topic for debate now. On the one hand, it has been argued that giving free stuff to the public is not a good practice. If freebies are given indiscriminately, the country's situation could deteriorate as it happened in Sri Lanka. On the other hand, it's been opined that if the tax paid by the people is used to give free things to the people, it is not wrong. As such, what is the impact of freebies culture on Indian society and its economy?

Welfare Schemes v Freebies

The freebie culture that prevails during the election has been regarded as "Revadi Culture" by Prime Minister Narendra Modi. Because of such reasons, at times, India has been called the 'Langar Nation.' However, Revadi and Langar's terms do not reflect the actual adverse effects of freebies culture. The intention of the political party behind freebies is only to gain votes.

Welfare measures are the policy interventions that have medium to long-term positive impacts on future production and productivity. For such reasons, they are also known as merit goods. Examples include, the Public Distribution System (PDS), several employment generation schemes like Mahatma Gandhi National Rural Employment Guarantee (MGNREGA), free Covid-19 vaccines, and free health and education for the weaker sections. All these are covered by welfare schemes which any responsible government does for the social upliftment of society.

On the contrary, any interventions without a medium to long-term positive impacts on future production and productivity are called freebies. These freebies are generally announced during elections, such as free electricity, free public transportation, free water, waiver of pending utility bills, and agricultural loans waiver. These kinds of popularisation promises are considered to be freebies.

The difference between the both is a tad tricky, but it can be understood by checking the ultimate goal of such policies or schemes. If measures are taken to fulfill the provisions of the Directive Principles of State Policy (DPSP), such as social justice, economic improvement, and future growth, then they are welfare schemes. On the contrary, if schemes focus on short-term benefits or are distributed as gifts, they are freebies with only votes as motivation. It can be said that Economic sensibility can only distinguish welfare measures and freebies.

Shortcomings of Freebies Culture

Although it is not a new instrument in Indian politics, its roots can be traced back to the 1960s subsidized rice for votes in the south Indian election and the 1970s Indira Gandhi's government populous regime. Still, the All India

Anna Dravida Munnetra Kazhagam (AIADMK) of Tamil Naidu gets the credit for converting freebies tactics into the mainstream; It promoted the distribution of free pressure cookers, sarees, washing machines, and television sets, among others, in exchange for votes. At the same time, Akali Dal promised free electricity in exchange for votes. Due to these high subsidies burden, during 2021-22, the Debt-to-GDP ratio reached 53.3 percent, the highest in the country.

Ever since this freebies culture was introduced to the mainstream, it has slowly hollowed the Indian economy and its political system. With every changing government, political parties make more economically unviable promises. The latest example being AAP announced Rs. 1000 per month to every woman during the Punjab election.

The Flip Side of the Welfare State

Freebies aren't for Free; to fulfill such populous promises government has to take funds from public funds, which are money collected as tax from the taxpayer of this country. According to a report by the RBI, freebies undermine credit culture and result in cross-subsidization. These freebies are the same as other subsidies, revenue expenditures fueled by State funds. It results in price dispersion and inflation, affects private investment, and has a worse effect on the labor force in the long run.

As per the report of CRISIL, "Most States are struck in Unsustainable Debt Situations due to the growing culture of freebies." As a result, the spending power to fund public welfare measures or merit goods is also negatively affected. For example, Punjab's electricity subsidy and rising cost to state exchange are 16 percent more than its total revenue. According to the RBI, the expenditure on freebies of different states is 0.1 percent to 2.7 percent of GSDP (Gross State Domestic Product).

These regressive measures of the political parties affect the financial discipline, banks' future loaning system, and state finances very poorly. It is not very hard to grasp the long-term effect of this constant emphasis on freebies is not just state funds but also causes a spiral of government debt which ultimately affects the growth and development of the country. The government depends on such freebies for votes rather than actual development and changes in the state. In FY 2021-22, Andhra Pradesh used 13 percent of its budget on Rs. 22,000 Crores for interest payments.

Public finances, which should be used as a capital investment in physical and social infrastructure, are instead being spent on such freebies to fulfill promises in the form of unplanned revenue expenditure. According to the RBI report and studies, since 2014, the social sector expenditure has decreased even after increased state shares in the finance commission and union budget. Also, there is a decline in critical sectors like health and education, which the state government is leading in funding.

The side effects of freebies such as free electricity are excess groundwater extraction, no climate-appropriate cropping pattern, soil erosion in the long term, a decrease in soil productivity, and, ultimately, lesser production.

How are a few Indian States on the verge of becoming Sri Lanka?

Numerous factors are responsible for the economic condition of Sri Lanka, such as unsustainable loans, a drop in the tourism-based economy, China's "Debt Trap" Policy, and poor financial planning, among others. The biggest reason behind Sri Lanka's economic crisis is President Gotabaya Rajapaksha's tax cut promises during the 2019 election campaign. After the election, Sri Lanka registered a salary increase of Rs 60,000 crore in annual revenue due to the provision of taxes from 15 percent to 8 percent without any financial outlook. Because of such frivolous promises and policies, the country has fallen into such an economic crisis that it is failing to fulfill the people's basic needs. Sri Lanka is on the verge of bankruptcy due to its destructive policies. In the past year, it is not confined to Sri Lanka only. Several countries, such as Venezuela, Cuba, and North Korea, have been victims of their economic ruin.

Recently, the RBI governor highlighted in his report that several of our Indian states are also on the same road toward severe economic crisis; conditions such as Punjab, Rajasthan, Bihar, Kerala, and West Bengal are at the top of the list. These states are the most indebted. The report also estimates that by 2026, the debt to GSDO ratio of some of these states in India could reach 35 percent, for which states relaxed tax policies, the state announced subsidies, and to fulfill freebies commitment withdrawals from state funds are responsible for such unsubstantiated expenditure.

Legal Position

Recently, Prime Minister Modi appealed to the youth of the country; not to fall for this "Revadi culture" but instead focus on their education and better future. These freebies are short-term instruments used to get votes in exchange for these complimentary goods and services. Even the previous Chief Justice of India, NV Ramana, directed the central government to draft a solid framework to control the freebies culture. Also, during a hearing of a PIL regarding this matter, the apex court bench suggested the finance commission formulate an effective measure against this freebies culture.

In 2013, the controversy reached the Supreme Court when a complaint was lodged against the Tamil Nadu government. The complaint claimed that the government was bribing the people. Section 123 of the Representation of the People Act deals with Bribery to either influence voters or induce someone to contest or withdraw from the election. But after hearing this case, the Supreme Court passed the landmark judgment that this does not amount to bribery. Giving freebies to people is different from bribing people. The Supreme Court suggested they either form an expert panel to evaluate the issue or call for an all-party meeting. The Court said there was a need to have an extensive hearing on this issue. The Supreme Court also directed the Election Commission to consult political parties and frame a guideline to curb the freebie culture.

In 2014, Election Commission made some guidelines for the model code of conduct. It was said that Parties could not make illogical promises to influence the voters. All the promises made in manifestoes must present a comprehensive plan to tackle the financial requirement and fulfill such promises. While in 2015, the Election Commission of India also ordered all the political parties to provide copies of their manifestoes.

Article 324 of the Indian Constitution allows the Election Commission to conduct free and fair elections. The Election Commission can suspend the party's recognition if it fails to follow the Model Code of Conduct (MCC).

Why has the Freebies Culture not been curbed?

Despite these efforts and guidelines, this freebie culture is at its peak. To curb this menace Election Commission of India needs more power and autonomy to implement the policies and track the actions of these political parties. However, Supreme Court intervention and Election Commission's demands are still not provided.

In 2014, the Election Commission sent 22 proposals to the c regarding electoral reforms that included the power to cancel the registration of political parties. Similarly, in 2016, a proposal was also sent to the Union Law Ministry seeking specific aid in powers to register political parties. It was demanded that along with the freebies in the manifestoes, it should also be told from where the resources would come to fulfill the promises. Unfortunately, due to political interference, these reforms were never implemented. Anyhow, the sadness of the central government on this issue can be seen. But still, concrete steps need to be taken to curb this issue.

Establishing a difference between welfare schemes and freebies is crucial to curb such a deteriorating culture. Despite all, in every upcoming election, all the political parties have started using financial resources to fuel their election campaign. It has taken the contour of who can bid how big for votes. The Chairperson of the 15th Finance Commission, N.K Singh, said, "Political competition over such sops (Standard operating procedure) is a quick passport to fiscal disaster."

Suggestions

COVID-19 has already hampered the growth of the economy. The focus must be on prudent spending, sound monetary policy, and fiscal consolidation before making any policy to improve the country's economic condition instead of distributing freebies.

The FRBM Act, 2003 (Fiscal Responsibility and Budget Management Act) needs to be amended to set limits on loan waivers, free electricity, and other subsidies. And Election commission should be provided with substantial powers and an effective monitoring system to eradicate this freebies culture effectively.

We need to develop an operational and financially sustainable economic system which is more efficient in using the resources at hand in health, infrastructure, education and much more that will also help in creating more jobs and help to attain social justice.

As the famous adage goes, 'Give a man a fish, and you feed him for a day, teach men to fish, and you feed him for a lifetime.' Political parties should focus on skill development and employment generation rather than relying on freebie culture and frame better policies so that India does not need to become a langar nation.

Conclusion

The paper illustrates that the freebie culture has been a consistent phenomenon in Indian politics. Moreover, the paper shows India's significant challenges in tackling the freebie culture. The existing measures available to the government proved inadequate to handle the problem posed by the freebie culture. The elections are the most critical factor that has encouraged the freebie culture in India. As such, the paper suggests that the FRBM Act needs to be strengthened, among other things, to tackle the freebie culture in India.

CHAPTER V

Understanding of Psycho-Criminological Mechanism

Written by Akhya Tewari (5th Semester, BA-Ewing Christian College, Prayagraj).

Introduction

Why do people commit crimes, and what could prevent them from doing so in the future? Is the objective of a criminal to set an example or is there a motive? The question of why people choose to commit crimes—often regardless of severe consequences—is at the root of criminal psychology. In the current world, we interrogate the connection between psychology and criminology. The primary aim is to investigate how mindsets about the nature of criminal behavior predict punitive and rehabilitative attitudes. The scientific study of the causes of crime in relation to man and society who set and define rules and regulations for himself and others to govern the study of crimes, causes of crimes, the meaning of crime in terms of law and community reaction to Crime. It that aims to explain the connection between crime and the personal characteristics of the offender including his environment

Psycho-criminology

Psycho-criminology perspectives are applied to understanding the causes of criminal behavior. It is viewed as the convergence of psychology and criminology within it concerns the use of psychological insight to define, illustrate and prevent criminal nature. It aims to survey by means of what individual criminal action is seized, stimulated, claimed, and changed through traits, social, and/or referring to practices or policies that do not negatively affect the environment. The use of these approaches in Forensic Psychiatry helps comprehend the causes of criminal or anti-social management and its connection accompanying welfare and mental disorders. Our discussion of the various dimensions of a concept may seem trivial, but its importance becomes clear when we consider what we mean by the concept of 'crime'. The subject matter of criminology (crime) is different from the subject matter of many other academic disciplines

Some individuals commit crimes out of necessity; others are driven by anger, rejection of authority, a manipulative personality, or psychopathic tendency. Over the years, a greater understanding of psychology, human behavior, and psychiatry has helped in bringing significant changes as to how the legal experts think about law, as well as changes, in how the criminal justice system treats the mentally ill persons. So far, extensive research points to a complex mix of genetics, personality, life circumstances, and environmental factors.Psychological and psychiatric findings have had a significant influence on the legal system, particularly since the beginning of the 20th century. Among meaningful changes involve the push towards deinstitutionalization of the mentally ill, which coincided with the development of more advanced psychiatric medications and a better understanding of the causes and potential treatments for mental disorders. Psychology and Crime comprehensively covers the dynamic role of psychological hypotheses and procedures in understanding and directing criminal behaviour. It analyzes in depth the request of psychological verdicts to a range of serious crimes, in the way that arson, violent crime, and sexual crime. It analyzes the use of psychology by the police and the courts and examines the function of psychology in crime reduction approaches.

Evolving concept

According to the theory of Merton R. K. 'Humans are fundamentally good people and conforming beings who are strongly influenced by values and attitudes of the society in which they live'. This theory assumes that humans are creatures of conformity who want to do the right thing. The right thing is what society considers to be right. Family, education, social network, and contacts' influence, can help access the right thing. When there is 'perceived discrepancy', between the goals cherished and materialist values and the availability of legitimate means, then delinquency and crime occur. Individuals and groups who experience a high level of strain are forced to decide whether to accept or violate laws or norms; consequently, they withdraw, conform or rebel.

By postulating and investigating such mechanisms, researchers have sought explanations of a wide range of psychological phenomena. However, the concept has been deployed in dramatically different ways, with very different meanings, depending upon the particular school or tradition of psychology (and specific research program therein). In fact, usage has been so diverse as to defy easy categorization or definition. But a historical perspective, even if rather selective, can trace the broad outlines of the significance of psychology.

Understanding psychology

Psychology is a step forward in making the legal system perfect, the role played by psychology in the legal system helps in modifying our legal system and also helps in maintaining justice, equity, and good conscience. The study of criminal psychology can help in preventing more crimes happening in future as the best way to reduce crime is to understand the criminal's mind.In most important inclusive sense, psychological mechanisms offer a type of new explanation of mental states and behavior, often with reference to underlying processes, systems, projects, or entities. By postulating and investigating such mechanisms, researchers have sought answers of a wide range of psychological phenomena. However, the concept has been deployed in dramatically different ways, accompanying very different intentions, revolving around the particular school or tradition of psychology (and specific research program therein). In fact, usage has been so various concerning defy easy classification or description.

Research plans that the semantic patterns of psychopaths are uniquely distinguished accompanying the patterns of non psychopaths. Their stylistic dissimilarities indicate how they view the world around them, as well as their deep emotional deficit and detachment from emotional events.However, psychopaths' lack of impression and sticking to others allows bureaucracy to have clearness in observing the nature of their prey. They do not get caught in or bogged down by the anxieties and emotions that other people experience in social situations.

Conclusion

Understanding the minds of psychopaths and their personality and behavioral traits allows experts to design strategies that more likely will work with authority. Psychopaths' scheming to manipulate nature can make it difficult for officers to get accurate information from them upon any less condition than the law enforcement interviewer has experienced in specific strategies for interrogating a psychopath. Professionals working in law enforcement, disciplines, and other security-accompanying professions must comprehend psychopathy and allure suggestions. Because of its relevance to police officers, adjustments, the courts, and others working in connected fields, the need to understand psychopathy cannot be exaggerated. This includes knowing by what method to identify psychopaths, the damage they can cause, and how to deal with them more effectively.

CHAPTER VI

Understanding the humanitarian situation and suppression abiding by Aryan Tribal race and ethnic people in the 21 century

Written by Tanushree (4th Semester, BA. LL.B - Chandigarh University, Mohali).

Abstract

William Jones, famously, by identifying close linkages between Sanskrit and European languages, gave birth to research into the common ancestry between Indians and Europeans. In the earlier years of contention on the matter, India was considered the cradle of civilisation and Sanskrit as the mother of all Indo-European languages. With the rise in the imperial power of Europe over India, the cradle of civilisation began to shift outside India and ultimately landed in Europe. Simultaneously, the idea of invasion of India by the 'Aryan race', or the Aryan invasion theory (AIT), was promoted. Since then, however, one archaeological find over another have consistently refuted the AIT, proving it as false.

Introduction

Have you ever wondered why Indian women place a red dot on their foreheads, between their eyes? In ancient times, a groom used to apply a spot of his blood on his bride's forehead in recognition of wedlock! At one time, the tilak, or bindi was a sign of a happily married woman. A single woman, or one who was a widow, did not wear the mark. While it remains a very old tradition and a sign of marriage, today it is much more of a fashion accessory. Today, the bindi can be any colour, shape or size, and women often wear more than one. The transformation in the use of the bindi is evidence that even old traditions can change over time. Things certainly changed in the Indus Valley when a new group called the Aryans arrived. The thorniest, most fought-over question in Indian history is slowly but surely getting answered: did Indo-European language speakers, who called themselves Aryans, stream into India sometime around 2,000 BC – 1,500 BC when the Indus Valley civilisation came to an end, bringing with them Sanskrit and a distinctive set of cultural practices.

As flawed as it remains, this theory has, nonetheless, persisted and morphed in its current form as the Aryan migration theory (AMT) and continues to find mention and favour in contemporary academic discourse. In mainstream academia, today, whether in grade-school texts or in texts meant for undergraduate and graduate study, whenever India and Hinduism are mentioned, the coming of Aryans from outside of India and establishing Hinduism and civilisation in India are discussed as veritable facts. By examining the theory in anticolonial and postcolonial contexts, we show that despite considerable archaeological evidence refuting the theories of the invasion or migration of Aryans into India, its colonial embeddedness in the notion of the racial superiority of the Europeans or people with European ancestry that the theory does not fade into oblivion.

Identification of Aryans

Aryans were associated with ethnicity and, especially, with light-skinned (Caucasian) superiority also Theories had been advanced earlier regarding a correlation between Sanskrit and European languages

Also "common source" via the Rig Veda and the history of the Indus Valley Civilisation created the myth of an Aryan Invasion of the region which claimed light-skinned Aryans conquered darker-skinned indigenous people and established high civilisation.

In the present day, the term is understood to properly refer to the early Indo-Iranian and Indo-Aryan migratory group, possibly originally from the region of the Ural River or, according to some scholars, to the Indo-Iranians only based on the continued usage of the term by the great Persian Empires of the near east. After a DNA research it was found that the 3 major groups that existed in the indian subcontinent in the ancient era were:

1 - South Asians were basically hunter-gatherers - the people who are the original inhabitants of the subcontinent who we would now connect to those like the Andaman islanders;

2 - Iranian agriculturalists who are believed to have brought farming of wheat & barley to the subcontinent;
3 - Steppe pastarolists or the inhabitants of the vast grasslands north of Afghanistan.

Then in the 2000 BCE, the steppe pastarolists whom we know as aryans moved downward in the subcontinent Alongwith south asian to known as ancestral South Indians. Whereas few of south asian stayed there with the steppe pastarolists to be known as Ancestral north Indians. Brahmins in north india were more likely to have steppe ancestryAryan invasion theory the migratory band of peoples later referred to as Indo-Iranians and Indo-Aryans came originally from the area of modern-day Kazakhstan near the Ural River and moved slowly toward the Iranian Plateau where they arrived sometime prior to the 3rd millennium BCE. Whatever they may have called themselves at this time is unknown, but they would later self-reference as Aryans, designating a class of people who were free, noble, and civilized as contrasted with those who did not share their values.

There is no evidence of a racial difference, only a class difference. The term seems to have been used in the same way one today might differentiate between high or low-class individuals. Opponents of the invasion theory make a somewhat plausible case that the sacrificial rites and rituals described in some of the Vedic texts bear a resemblance to practices that may have been common during the Harappan period. The similarity between Harappan and Vedic altars is indeed intriguing. This would bolster the argument that Brahmins of the Vedic age emerged from the Harappan priesthood, and not from any Aryan invasion. But a link between the Harappan priesthood and Vedic Brahminism does not preclude the possibility of an invasion or foreign migration. It is not inconceivable that the Vedic Brahmin developed as a composite of the Harappan priest and the priest of an invading (or migrating) tribe or clan. Animal sacrifices were common amongst many tribes in that age - and it is not entirely implausible that some kind of synthesis may have taken place.

Aryan migration theory

At some point, the so-called Indo-Aryans of the original migratory group went south toward India where they are thought to have merged with the indigenous people of the Indus Valley Civilization (also known as the Harappan Civilization or Harappan Culture, c. 7000 - c. 600 BCE). This civilization was highly advanced as evidenced by Neolithic sites such as Mehrgarh, occupied prior to 7000 BCE, whose populace developed agricultural techniques, religious rituals, domestication of plants and animals, and produced impressive artistic works.

By c. 2600 BCE, the great cities of Harappa, Mohenjo-daro, Ganeriwala, and over 1,000 others had risen, the ruins of which give evidence of advanced urban planning and technological skill. These cities had running water and a highly developed sewer and drainage system which directed rainwater or waste toward fixtures on either side of the streets. Homes were constructed in such a way as to cut down on outside noises and were built with "wind catchers" which provided air conditioning within; a luxury not even Rome, at its height, developed. The people of the Indus Valley also created a writing system (as yet undeciphered), musical instruments, farming implements, and large, flat-bottomed boats. Ports were constructed with great warehouses for goods and trade was conducted with a number of other nationalities, notably the people of Mesopotamia and Egypt.

At some point between c. 1900 - c. 1500 BCE, the Indus Valley Civilization began to decline. Cities were abandoned and there was a significant migration of the people toward the south of the subcontinent. This period of migration and change coincides with the development of Vedic thought and the so-called Vedic Period (c. 1500 - c.500 BCE) when the vedas, the sacred texts of Hinduism, were committed to written form in Sanskrit. Since the people of the Indus Valley Civilization did not write in Sanskrit, this language – and the concepts it expressed in the scriptures – had to have come from somewhere else. It is thought that they arrived with an Indo-Aryan migration.

Indus valley civilisation

The Indus Valley Civilisation is thought to have been a Bronze Age civilisation that spanned from modern-day northwest India and northeast Pakistan to western Tibet. The discovery of the Indus Valley Civilisation was first made in the 1920s by archaeologists John Marshall, Ernest Mackay, and Harold Hargreaves. While excavating the site of Harappa in what is now Pakistan, they found evidence of an ancient civilisation that was far more advanced than anything they had seen before. The Indus Valley Civilisation is thought to have been the most technologically advanced of all the early civilisations.

The civilisation was first identified in 1921 at Harappa in the Punjab region and then in 1922 at Mohenjodaro, near the Indus river in the Sindh region. The civilisation of the industry is known to the archaeologists as the Harappa culture The three cities in it are harappa, mohenjodaro, kalibanga. The origins of the harappa culture has recently been thrown by the excavations of Kot diji, opposite mohenjodaro a few miles from the left of the Indus. Here below the level of the harappa culture have been found remains of an earlier culture with poetry and tools of crude workmanship. This kot diji culture seems to have been the prototype of the developed city civilization which grew out of it.

Dravidian

Some people claim that the Dravadians originally inhabited the Northern part of India and were later pushed to the southern part of the country by the Aryans. Hence about 28% of Indians are Dravidians and reside in South India with one of the Dravadian languages as their main language, which includes, Tamil, Malayalam, Telugu, Kannada and Tulu. The Dravidian language has three subgroups, namely North Dravidian, Central Dravidian and South Dravidian. In present-day India, the states of Andhra Pradesh, Karnataka, Kerala and Tamil Nadu are the significant regions with a Dravidian population, the rest 72% are Aryans, residing in North India. The difference in the origin of these languages is the reason of the different South and North Indian accents. We know very little about the Dravidian people in India, who used to reside in the country before the Aryans invaded Northern India from Iran and Southern Russia.

Dravidian people residing in present-day Central India are tribal people known as Gond people, Kannadigaru Dravidians are from Karnataka, northern Kerala and southern Maharashtra, and northwest Tamil Nadu, Kondha Dravidians are from eastern Indian states of Andhra Pradesh and Orissa, Kodavas Dravidian people from Karnataka and northern Kerala. Then there are Kurukh, Malayali, Tamil, Telugus and Tuluvas people who belong to Dravidians in India.

As per sources, these people migrated from Africa and reached South India via the southern route about 50,000 years ago. Because of rivers and fertile soil they stayed in India in large numbers, than other parts of world.

It is said that Dravidians were: Farmers and richly settled people.

With the coming of the Aryans, the concept of heaven and God came into existence which dramatically changed society.

Factual gene evidence

R1a is distributed all over Europe, Central Asia and South Asia; its sub-group Z282 is distributed only in Europe while another subgroup Z93 is distributed only in parts of Central Asia and South Asia; and three major subgroups of Z93 are distributed only in India, Pakistan, Afghanistan and the Himalayas. This clear picture of the distribution of R1a has finally put paid to an earlier hypothesis that this haplogroup perhaps originated in India and then spread outwards. This hypothesis was based on the erroneous assumption that R1a lineages in India had huge diversity compared to other regions, which could be indicative of its origin here. As Prof. Richards puts it, “the idea that R1a is very diverse in India, which was largely based on fuzzy microsatellite data, has been laid to rest” thanks to the arrival of large numbers of genomic Y-chromosome data.

Conclusion

Indus civilization of the third millennium BCE, left behind exquisitely carved seals and thousands of short inscriptions in a long-forgotten pictographic script. Visual evidence like seals and inscribed Indus objects are analyzed in detail by Parpola. One may not know enough to follow some arguments, but the tracing back of certain themes to Mesopotamian ones, the decipherment of the fish and star. The fact that even such uncommon Indus symbols as the palm squirrel, which have a narrow pictorial meaning, find a natural and fitting explanation within a Dravidian linguistic framework is a hopeful sign.

Also, it confirmed the following-

- The Indus Civilization is chronologically earlier than the Vedic culture.
- The route and timing of Aryan immigration into South Asia can no longer be seriously disputed.
- Indo-Aryan and Dravidian have merged millennia ago to form the roots of Hinduism and sustain the continuity of Indian historical tradition till the present day.

CHAPTER VII

Tracing the Evolution of the Right to Die: Euthanasia

Written by Madhur Vashishtha (2nd Semester, BA. LL.B - Chandigarh University, Mohali).

Abstract

The "Right to die" has undergone a series of controversies by way of the common law jurisprudence of India right from being granted to being revoked and at present stands at a mid-spot between being existent and being non-existent i.e., 'Right to die' enjoys a partial existence in the contemporary Indian common law jurisprudence. This paper aims at exploring the jurisprudential development of the "Right to die" taking a holistic view of the right in its relation to the existent legal provisions and doctrines.

Keywords: Euthanasia, Right to Life, Right to Die, Article 21, Doctrine of Non-Waiver.

Introduction

Dictionary Meaning of Euthanasia is basically ending a Life Intentionally to Relieve Suffering and Pain. The Origin of Word "Euthanasia" comes straight out of Greek Language—"Eu", means Good or Well + "thanatos", means Death together adds up as "Good Death" or mercy killing."Right to live" has always been understood to be inclusive of the 'Right to die" since times immemorial, but with the evolution of state, the "Right to die" and "Right to live" came to be separated from each other as the life of an individual came to be viewed not just as his own but also of the state and on that philosophy it was envisaged that "Right to live" need not be taken as inclusive of "Right to die" and the latter (Right to die) was not just a right subjected to the discretion of the individual but also subjected to the discretion of the state. Thus, the "Right to die" was conditional to the state's approval. But, with the evolution of the current view of "Inalienable Rights" also known as 'Fundamental rights' or "Human rights" this 'Right to die' once again went on a jurisprudential evolution. As, Right to life was embedded as the basic fundamental right in the constitution and was made inalienable even by the state, the state lost its older say it had in the life of the individual. However, it (the state) still continued to be the guarantor of the right.

Classification of Euthanasia

1. Voluntary Euthanasia (with the consent of the patient): In Voluntary Euthanasia Patient's consent is necessary to perform it. It is already legal in some countries like Netherlands, Belgium, etc.

2. Non-Voluntary Euthanasia (consent of the patient is unavailable): when a person is not in the position to give his/her consent (for e.g. –the patient is in the state of severely brain-damaged or permanent vegetative state) and another person takes decisions on behalf of the patient, often the ill person had expressed a wish previously to end their life in such circumstances.

3. Involuntary Euthanasia (Against the will of the patient): Conducted Euthanasia against the will of the patient or without asking patient's consent is termed as involuntary euthanasia. It is also regarded as murder.

Types of Euthanasia can be further divided into Active and Passive Euthanasia

a) Active Euthanasia: Where a person intentionally intervenes to end someone's life with the use of lethal forces or substances. For example- The use of lethal injections to end life.

b) Passive Euthanasia: When a person causes death by withdrawing treatment that is essential to maintain life. For example- Removal of the life support system (Ventilator).

Jurisprudential evolution of the right to die

As already stated that "The Right to life" was embedded as a Fundamental right in the constitution under Article-21 and with such inclusion of it in the realm of fundamental right, it was made inalienable right of the citizens and the state lost its earlier say in the life of the individual. Once again, Right to life was viewed to be inclusive of the right to die and came to be viewed as one and the same and this view was also upheld by the Supreme Court in the case of "P. Rathinam V Union of India" – I am the Master of my Fate, I am the Captain of my Soul. This Statement was said by William Earnest Henley. In this Case Petitioner appeals to make Section 309 of Indian Penal Code (IPC) unconstitutional because it Violates Article 14 & 21 of the Indian Constitution. Section 309 of IPC, 1860, lays down the Provision for an Attempt to Commit Suicide as an Offence. Petitioner said, Mental Help is to be provided to a Person who Attempts Suicide in Place of Giving Punishment to Him. There are some important Statements given by Justice R.A. Jahagirdgar of Bombay High Court i.e. 1. Neither Academicians nor Jurists are Agree on what Constitute Suicide. 2. Mens Rea, without which even no Offence can be sustained. 3. Temporary Insanity is the Reason of such Acts, which is a Valid Defence, even in homoicides. He said Economic, Religion, Socio-Economic are may be the reasons to do Suicide and it is cruel or irrational to punish someone who has attempt to do suicide. In this case, after considering all the facts Supreme Court declares Section 309 of IPC Unconstitutional.

However, this view was taken aback by the Supreme Court in the case of "Gian kaur vs. Union of India": In this case, Gian Kuar and her husband Harbans Singh were convicted by the trail under Section 306 of IPC i.e. Abetment to Suicide. Kulwant Kuar was the lady who was helped by Gian and her husband to attempt Suicide. She was daughter-in-law of Gian Kaur. When case came in Supreme Court, Gian's lawyer said Section 306 of IPC is unconstitutional because 2 years earlier Section 309 of IPC was held unconstitutional in case of P. Rathinam V. Union of India. He also said due to the declaration of article 309 unconstitutional, Right to Death is our Fundamental Right and so it is our Fundamental Right, Helping someone to get their Fundamental Right is not to be Punishable. Justice mentioned that Article 21 is a positive concept; it does not include right to death, by this statement Supreme Court Overruled the P. Rathinam case of year 1994. Supreme Court also said "No Person has right on His/her life; only society has right on his life. Justice passed the Judgement and declared Section 306 and 309 of IPC constitutional and Right to Life does not include Right to Death.

However, with the definition of Life given by Supreme Court in the case of 'Francis Coralin Mullin V. Union of India', "Life is not just mere animal existence but it implies the right to live with Dignity". With the inclusion of Dignity in the ambit of life, the definition of life was widened. Life came to be viewed as no life at all without dignity and as such the question that rose was-

"CAN THERE BE RIGHT TO DIE, IF LIFE IS DEPRIVED OF DIGNITY? This question was answered in the affirmative by the Supreme Court in the "Aruna Shanbag Case" wherein it established a mid-viewpoint between both the extreme rights of "Right to live" and "Right to die". "Aruna Shanbag was a nurse in King Edward Memorial Hospital (KEM). On 27 November 1973, she was raped by sweeper in the basement. Sweeper Strangulated Aruna by dog chain, due to which oxygen couldn't reach Aruna's brain and she got brain damage &; she went into a permanent vegetative state (also called coma). - in 2009, Aruna was in coma for the last 36 years, Pinky Virani who was a Journalist and Social Activist, filed a writ petition in Supreme Court by using Article 32 and asked court to allow Passive Euthanasia to her because she has no chances of revival. For this Supreme Court appointed 3 doctors to get their opinion on this, after the investigation doctors submitted to the Court that Aruna is not brain dead, she can understand things & Euthanasia is not necessary. There are 3 Legal issues in front of the Supreme Court. First, should withdrawal of life sustaining systems and mean for a person who is in Permanent Vegetative State (PVS), be permissible? Second, if a person declares previously that he/she does not want to have life sustaining measures in case of futile care or a PVS, should her wishes be respected in such a situation? Third is- can the family or next of kin of a person make a request on behalf of a patient to withdraw life sustaining systems, in case a patient herself has not placed such a request previously?

The division bench, relying on doctor's report held that Aruna was not brain dead and since she could feel and understand things, Passive Euthanasia should not allowed to her. Bench said that Pinky Virani is not the next friend of Aruna Shanbag. Only KEM Hospital can be her next to friend. Bench also agreed that in some cases Passive Euthanasia maybe granted but with some guidelines i.e. application will be filed in High Courts for Passive Euthanasia. The Chief Justice of the High Court should constitute a bench of atleast 2 Judges,*The bench before laying out any judgement should consider the opinion of a committee of 3 reputed doctors,*It is also the duty of the court to issue a notice to state, relatives, kids and friends also provide them with the copy of the report made by the committee of the doctors. After hearing all the sides, the court should deliver the judgement *This procedure is followed in India until any legislation is passed
on the subject.

Conclusion

The Right to die although seems to be a right of contemporary relevance has however, has had a long history of its own and it is that very history that has built the foundation for this right in its contemporary relevance this paper has traced the right through its history all the way to its contemporary jurisprudential and legal stand. The right cannot be granted in its holistic form as the grant of it would defeat the doctrine of non-waiver and might serve as an encouragement to suicide. The evolution of this right can be summed up as "EXISTENT" to "NON- EXISTENT" to the present mid-stand between being "EXISTENT" to "NON- EXISTENT".

References

Is There a Right to Die - A Study of the Law of Euthanasia 3 Cumberland-Samford Law Review 1972 (heinonline.org)

R. Rathinam/N. Patnail v. Union of India - JT 1994 (3) SC 392 Case Comments 7 Student Advocate 1995 (heinonline.org)

Gian Kaur v. State of Punjab: Case Comment 18 Supremo Amicus 2020 (heinonline.org)

Aruna Ramchandra Shanbaug v Union of India and Others on 07 March 2011 - Judgement - LawyerServices

COMMON CAUSE VS UNION OF INDIA (researchgate.net)

Right to Life and Personal Liberty Under the Constitution of India: A Strive for Justice by Himangshu Ranjan Nath:: SSRN

CEEOL - Article Detail

CHAPTER VIII

Legal Framework to Protect the Rights of IDPS (Internally Displaced Persons): The Middle East and Africa

Written by Piyush Pandey (6th Semester, BA. LL.B - Chandigarh University, Mohali) & Sejal Mehendiratta (6th Semester, BA. LL.B - Chandigarh University, Mohali).

Introduction

We have all heard about refugees and the significant attention given to them by UNHCR and the United Nations Human Rights Council, but do we know what "internally displaced people," or refugees, are?

Unlike refugees, who cross an international border and are governed by the 1951 Convention relating to the status of refugees or the 1969 Convention dealing with specific aspects of refugee problems in Africa, internally displaced persons are not governed by any Conventions and are prone to greater vulnerability than refugees.

The African Union Convention for the Protection And Assistance of Internally Displaced Persons (Popularly referred to as the Kampala Convention) defines Internally Displaced Persons as "persons or groups of persons who have been forced or obliged to flee or to leave their homes or places of habitual residence, in particular as a result of or to avoid the effects of

- Armed conflicts
- Natural or Human-made disasters
- Situations of generalized conflicts

Human rights violations and those who have not crossed an internationally recognized border. These violations of human rights are prevalent in Africa on a large scale. Near-internal displacement accounts for nearly half of the total of 18 million displaced people. displaced people. by the Concerned Nations, the Views of UNHCR, and the Collaborative Approaches of Different Agencies in the World.

What Are the Measures Taken by the Concerned Nations When the Internal Displacement takes place due to:-

Armed Conflict

In Syria, there is no safe place to return. As the Syrian government continued its military offensives against non-state armed groups in its nine-year civil war, nearly 1.8 million people were recorded as displaced in 2019, compared to 2.9 million and 1.6 million in 2017 and 2018, respectively. Turkey's incursions became a major challenge for the people who were trying to return to their homes in north-eastern and north-western Syria.

Owing to these events, the Syrian Government implemented Law 10, which affirmed the redesigning of illegal housing areas and the expedition of land for reconstruction. But these measures are inadequate in the depth of Syria's ongoing crisis, of which the refugees and internally displaced people continue to bear the brunt.

In Yemen, 398,000 new displacements took place in 2019 as a result of conflict and violence. These displacements were not new; however, they escalated the vulnerabilities of the people. Efforts made to reach a political solution brought some relief as, in May 2018, the fighting began to withdraw. The Stockholm Agreement in December 2018 established a demilitarized zone around Hodeida, Yemen's main port. Restrictions were eased by Riyadh on Yemen's airspace so people could flow out of the capital to seek medical treatment abroad.

Environmental or human-made causes

Iran has been particularly hard hit by natural disasters. In 2019, 520,000 people were recorded as being internally displaced, the highest figure in the region to date. Torrential rains and floods caught people and the water management authorities by surprise. as it comes after a long (37,000-day) period of drought.

Similarly, in Iraq, 37,000 internal displacements were triggered by storms and flooding. Water scarcity is a major problem in Iraq. The country has an extensive network of dams and canals that provide irrigation facilities to semi-arid areas, which might have contributed to increasing the flood risk. These annual problems have not been dealt with by the government.

Lack of Development Opportunities

The Kampala Convention doesn't recognize this factor as a cause of internal displacement. It is estimated that by the year 2050, one out of four people of working age will be African. However, the sluggish growth of the employment sector has failed to keep pace with the rapid growth of labor, including both skilled and unskilled workers. The migration is predominately a south-south movement, particularly the refugees, who are moving to the sub-regions, especially West and Southern Africa, due to the armed conflicts in Central Africa.

Nigeria, the Democratic Republic of the Congo, and Sudan currently account for the largest number of displaced people. Their placement put a large amount of pressure on the already scarce resources of the poor communities, which gave rise to conflicts, environmental disasters, civil unrest, oppressive regimes, and abuse of human rights. This further increases the vulnerabilities of the poor people who turn to unsafe channels, with no hope for further improvement. The refugee crisis comes under the ambit of international law, but as the migration takes place inside the country, only the concerned nations can be dealt with as a crisis, and the measures taken by the African Union are discussed hereunder.

What are The Views of UNHCR?

The United Nations High Commissioner for Refugees has taken into account the needs of the internally displaced and taken practical and necessary steps in dire situations to protect their human rights. The UNHCR's Strategic Directions for 2017-2021 deserve special attention here. It elaborates the five main areas in which the office will put special attention on

- Centrality of Protection
- Promoting Incursions and self-reliance
- Responding in Emergencies and beyond
- Empowerment of People
- Pursuit of Solutions

However, in ground reality, UNHCR operations need further consideration. As per the findings, protection is unevenly integrated with operations. It doesn't always fully capitalize on its leadership of national clusters of protection. However, let us look at its role in the humanitarian crisis in the Middle East and Africa.

Syria

Due to the ongoing conflicts, people's vulnerabilities were on the rise. The pressures on the host countries were increasing as the conflict in the Syrian Arab Republic persisted. Around 70 percent of households in Lebanon were living below the poverty line. A total of 12.2 million people needed humanitarian support, of whom 7.6 million were IDPs. The UNHCR continued the implementation of its 2015 Strategic Response Plan for the Syrian Arab Republic. It used all the possible means to maximize the delivery of assistance and protection, including camp management, non-food items, and shelter, as authorized by the United Nations Security Council Resolutions 2139, 2165, and 2191.

Iraq

The security situation in Iraq was particularly severe in 2015. As new conflicts arose, so did the internal displacements. It is estimated that nearly 1 million civilians were displaced, which was a 50 percent increase in Iraq's internally displaced people in 2014.

The UNHCR and its partners continued to monitor checkpoints to assess the needs of IDPs and fleeing civilians. It also played the role of a leading authority in providing camp management, shelter, nonfood items, and protection to IDPs. Along with that, it provided cash assistance programs to the vulnerable IDPs, conducted protection training programs, and set up call centers to provide assistance and technical information to them.

Yemen

The country's complex humanitarian crisis was exacerbated by ongoing airstrikes, armed clashes, and shelling. What made it even more challenging was the lack of security while delivering the necessities to the 80 percent of the Yemeni population that receives humanitarian assistance. However, the UNHCR assists people by providing life-saving aid, legal assistance, and resettling processing.

The UNHCR has made considerable progress in achieving the gloits strategic priorities. It made significant progress by providing durable solutions. It worked on resettlement processing, as evidenced by the fact that 135,000 places for Syrian refugees were obtained by the end of 2016. With the help of the United Nations Development Program, the UNHCR launched the Regional Refugee and Resilience Plan in response to the Syrian crisis. Apart from this, it led to strategic partnerships with significant organizations in the Middle East and Africa to make generous contributions to support its operations and address the displacement challenges.

How the Kampala Convention acts as a breakthrough to address the rights of Internally Displaced People?

In 1992, to cope with the problems of IDPS, the UN Commission on Human Rights appointed an independent expert, Mr. Francis Deng, to examine the existing international standards on human rights, humanitarian law, and refugee law and their viability for the internally displaced.

The Representative, after studying it, submitted a non-binding document in 1998 titled "Guiding Principles on Internal Displacement." "Displacement" refers to the current gap in the international laws for the protection of IDPs in all three countries and after the displacement. This document is meant to guide the state, the international, and all the other relevant authorities in the protection of IDPS.

However, a major breakthrough came when the African Union decided to draft a treaty focused specifically on internally displaced people in 2004. A draft text was discussed and finalized in 2008 after the meeting of a group of experts in Addis Ababa in 2006.This draft act serves as a signal to the African Union that they are concerned about the internal displacement crisis and intend to take action.

The Kampala Convention came into effect in 2012, which represents more progress made by the AU as compared to the previous legal frameworks. It created a binding framework to work for African specialties in cases of internal displacement. The Convention was the first time that the States were involved in drafting a whole set of standards regarding IDPs. It also conveys that the African States see the problem of internal displacement as an issue of international concern if not dealt with properly. The Convention also acknowledges the African Union's responsibility to assist states in protecting the rights of IDPS.

The problem caused by the development projects is overlooked by the states while considering the internal displacement crisis. The number of people uprooted by development projects is higher than the number of displacements caused by armed conflicts. Forced displacements can also trigger internal strife within a community regarding the control of land and resources.

However, the Kampala Convention has reversed this ignorance and addressed this issue in Article 10 of the Convention. It states that the States will take all measures to prevent internal displacement caused by the development projects and will explore alternatives with full consultation and information for the people who may be displaced.

This cause of displacement, however, was addressed only in the draft text and was not mentioned in the final text. But the elimination of references to displacement caused by a lack of development is appropriate. As discussed above, a lack of employment and opportunity is one of the reasons for internal displacement. This is because some people leave their villages voluntarily to seek opportunities outside of their area. However, it didn't take into account the lack of opportunities as a factor because, considering that, it really oversimplified the concept of internal displacement.

Another area that demands considerable attention is the responsibility of non-state actors in causing internal displacement. The root cause of displacement in Africa can possibly be traced back to domestic conflicts. The United Nations Human Rights Law doesn't recognize the question of whether these non-state actors can commit violations of human rights; however, if a legal position is drawn outlining their liabilities, it seems unlikely that these armed groups would consider themselves bound. The issue also seems to be differently addressed in the final text and draft text. The Convention also didn't afford legal status to these armed groups

What were The Collaborative Approaches of Different Agencies around the World?

World Bank

In 2016, the World Bank contributed $250 million to support the communities hosting displaced people, particularly in the Democratic Republic of the Congo, Ethiopia, Uganda, and Zambia. Creating both short-term and long-term opportunities in the eastern province of Congo can help improve the social contract between the government and the citizens for a peace process.

UNDP

The UNDP has also advanced human development approaches in addressing internal displacement. With the goal of the 2030 Development Agenda, the UNDP recommends the dating of the IASC Framework on durable solutions as a framework offor whole o-of-ciety approach. It also suggested promoting resilience-based development and prosperity for all. Municipalities should be supported to plan for the displaced people coming into their communities. It also states that it will focus on integrated solutions in order to address the stalled position of internal displacement.

Conclusion

The crisis of internal displacement is far from over. The primary responsibility for providing support and protection to internally displaced people rests with the governments of the nations where they are found, which is an essential component of sovereignty. The role of the global community is complementary. No one agency or organization has been named the global leader in the protection and aid of internally displaced people on a global scale. Instead, everyone is urged to work together to meet these requirements in accordance with the "collaborative method." It is generally acknowledged that more work has to be done to assist the displaced. The approach as a whole is utterly inadequate for a problem of this size. The international response has been hampered by serious operational gaps in the UN and agency responses to IDPs' needs, especially their protection, and ongoing budget challenges.

References

https://journals.sagepub.com/doi/full/10.1177/00438200221104498

https://www.icvanetwork.org/uploads/2022/04/Chapter-Global-Protection-Cluster-Handbook-for-the-Protection-of-Internally-Displaced-Persons-Part-1-The-Legal-Framework-for-the-Protection-of-Internally-Displaced-Persons.pdf

https://emergency.unhcr.org/entry/250553/idp-definition

https://www.ohchr.org/en/special-procedures/sr-internally-displaced-persons/about-internally-displaced-persons

https://rm.coe.int/baseline-coe-report-on-idp-/16808c9da5

https://blogs.kcl.ac.uk/kslr/wp-content/blogs.dir/86/files/2017/12/7-Nafees-Ahmad.pdf

https://www.ncbi.nlm.nih.gov/pmc/articles/PMC9356202/

https://digitalcommons.du.edu/cgi/viewcontent.cgi?article=1184&context=djilp

https://www.physio-pedia.com/International_Legislation_Governing_Forced_Displacement

https://www.unhcr.org/5cd569877.pdf

CHAPTER IX

An Implementation of Ideology in Equity

Written by Shashank Shekhar Bhardwaj (6th Semester, BA. LL.B - Chandigarh University, Mohali).

Abstract

"An idea is something you have; an ideology is something that has you"— Morris Berman

Ideology refers to a set of interrelated ideas dealing with politics, society, and the economy. In an effort to justify, explain, contest, or alter the social and political structures and procedures of a political society, a political ideology is a collection of ideas, beliefs, values, and views that compete over offering action plans for public policy-making. Ideological concepts are open to partially contradictory conceptual interpretations. The first views ideology as imposed on a community and abstract, closed, and dogmatic, mostly oblivious to empirical data. The second views ideology as a collection of behaviorally observable attitudes toward political matters that can be studied empirically. The third see ideologies as key resources for comprehending and influencing socio-political life because they serve as an essential mapping mechanism of cultural symbols and political notions. They vie for control over the "proper" and valid interpretations of political terms and concepts, ultimately contesting for the political high ground.

Introduction of Ideology

An ideology is a set of beliefs and values attributed to a person or group of persons, especially as held for reasons that are not purely epistemic. According to Charles P. Schleicher. "An ideology is a system of abstract ideas held by an individual (or group) which purports to explain reality, expresses value goals, and contains programs of action for the rejection or attainment of the kind of social order in which its proponents believe the goals can best be realized."Political Ideologies are very important in any State, Political ideologies tell about the nature of the Nation it describes the relationship between the state and society. From a social-scientific viewpoint, an ideology is a more or less coherent set of ideas that provides a basis for organized political action, whether this is intended to preserve, modify or overthrow the existing system of power relationships. All ideologies, therefore, offer an account of the existing order, usually in the form of a 'world view', providing a model of a desired future, a vision of a good society, and outlining how political change can and should be brought about. Ideologies are not hermetically sealed systems of thought; instead, they are fluid sets of ideas that overlap with one another at a number of points.

Meaning And Origin Of The Term Ideology

The French philosopher Destutt de Tracy coined the term ideology in 1796. In order to understand the beginnings of conscious thought and ideas, he utilized it to describe a new science of ideas. However, the phrase was given a more permanent connotation in the nineteenth century by Karl Marx. Marx believed that ideology was nothing more than the ideas of the ruling class system, which supported exploitation.

Political Ideology of India

If we discuss India, we see that India has been inclusive of ideologies since ancient times. The polity of India has successfully completed the journey of democracy through monarchy. From the Mughal period to the British and after the revolution of 1857, scholars and supporters of many ideologies in India started saying their own words and supporting them. The political Ideology of India is mainly socialist and liberal, but there are people who believe in and support other ideologies like communism, capitalism, conservatism, etc. in India. The Constitution of India declares India to be mainly a secular socialist ideology.

The ideology of Political Parties in India

1. Congress

Congress was established in 1885. The purpose of the establishment of Congress was to awaken new consciousness in the Indian public. Congress was established as a national party, synonymous with nationalism apart from regional and religious politics. Socialism was the ideology of Congress. It can be clearly seen that Congress has mainly established itself as a Nationalist Secular Secularist party devoid of regionalism. Since its inception, the ideology of Congress has kept on changing with time. Two ideologies in Congress at the time of the independence movement. Out of which one was of extreme nationalism and the other cannot be said of complete nationalism. After getting independence, Congress leaders presented themselves and the party as a secular nationalist and socialist party. People accepted the initial ideology of Congress. And he got the support of the people of the whole country, but in today's era, the people of Congress ideology have rejected the Congress party on Indian politics for 25 years from 1947. Some socialist plans, mixed economy, five-year plans, agriculture, irrigation, etc should be given priority through the Planning Commission; some important land reforms will have to be done to reach the board.

2. Bharatiya Janata Party

The Bharatiya Janata Party emerged as a constituent of the Jan Sangh. The Bharatiya Janata Party made socialism the basis of its ideology, but soon it made the politics of religion and conservatism the center of its politics. Together, Ram Janmabhoomi was included in its election manifesto, along with this, the Bharatiya Janata Party traveled to the pinnacle of Indian politics by keeping the ideologies of Hindutva, conservatism, etc. at the center. Simultaneously, in 15 states, BJP is running the government with a full majority or allies.

3. Communist Party

The Russian Revolution mainly influenced the Communist ideology in India. The Communist Party of India was formed in 1925. The Communist Party also participated in the Indian independence movement. In 1964, the Communist Party split and the Communist Party Marxist was formed. They have elected representatives in some states including Kerala and there is a full majority government in Kerala. If we look at the scenario of India, communist ideology has increased in many parts. In some places, communist ideology is linked to Karl Marx and in some places, Communism is said to be inspired by Lenin, Mao, and Stalin. The meaning of communism is mainly sociopolitical, philosophical, and economic ideology, but in today's era, the main objective of the communist parties is to oppose the government through war and to remove the government.

Implementation of ideology

India is a country with a multi-party system. It is a confluence of many ideologies. In our country, the government is elected through elections in a democratic system, in order to win these elections, parties put forward different ideas, and different types of election promises are made. India In view of this, it can be said that there are different types of ideologies in the whole country, and political parties keep making populist promises to win the elections. Today there is a need to spread any ideology evenly across the country. People who believe in different ideologies like communism, capitalism, socialism, conservatism, nationalism, etc. live all over the country. India is a union of states. And the ideology of that party can be clearly seen in the speeches of the leaders. Generally, we see that parties are implementing ideology in elections on the basis of the state and its culture. Which party justifies any one issue in 1 state the same thing is wrong in another state? For example, if we look at a party that justifies eating beef in one state while eating beef in another state is downright wrong. In our country, ideologies vary from place to place. Parties like Congress or BJP, which started politics with socialist ideology, today are doing politics just to win elections by moving away from their ideology. At the same time, the Communist Party and other regional parties are also doing the politics of appeasement and communalism, and regionalism, instead of doing politics of ideology.

Conclusion

So long as you do not achieve social liberty, whatever the law provides freedom is of no avail to you. B. R. Ambedkar. Ideology plays an important role in the welfare and development of the state. Today, Indian political parties need to move away from electoral politics to politics of ideology, politics of sect and religion is a big threat to the unity, integrity, and sovereignty of India. Today Ideology is talked about only in the speeches of leaders and in election rallies. There is a need for change in that, we need to become a socialist, public welfare, liberal, secular state as per the definition of the constitution. Leaders and political parties need to take their ideologies to the people on the ground. We can become the country of dreams of leaders like Gandhi, Ambedkar, Bhagat Singh, and Deendayal Upadhyay in the true sense only by making students study and research various political thinkers.

No matter where you stand politically- even if you're unsure of what your political ideology is - it is important to take part in the process of shaping our government.- Brad Henry

Reference

Book-INDIA'S STRUGGLE FOR INDEPENDENCE- Bipin Chandra, Mridula Mukharjee, Aditya Mahajan, K.N. Panikkar,

Book- Ambedkar's India by B.R. Ambedkar

Book- Nationalism by R.N.Tagore

https://www.sciencedirect.com/topics/psychology/political-ideology

ttps://www.thehindu.com/books/books-reviews/indian-politics-congress-political-party ideology/article65992339.ece

CHAPTER X

Is our society really inclusive of women?

Written by Yuni Basnet (2nd Semester, BA. LL.B - Chandigarh University, Mohali).

Introduction

A prohibition on menstruating women (those between the ages of 10 and 50) entering the well-known Sabarimala Sree Dharma Sastha Shrine, a temple devoted to Lord Ayyappa was sought in 1990. In its ruling in S. Mahendran v. The Secretary, Travancore, the High Court of Kerala prohibited their admittance on the grounds that the aforementioned exclusion was constitutional and reasonable since it was a long-standing practise that had existed since the dawn of time (1993).

The focus of the analysis is the Supreme Court's decision, which favoured constitutional morality over these traditions. Menstruating women between the ages of 10 and 50 were prohibited from accessing the Sabarimala shrine. The limitations and their origin stem from the concept that Swami Ayyappa, the temple god, is a "Naishtika Brahmachari" (celibate) and, as such, an epitome of cleanliness that should not be breached by menstruating women. Due to this, women are prohibited from visiting the Sabarimala temple grounds under Rule 3(b) of the Kerala Hindu Places of Public Worship (Authorization of Entry) Rules, 1965.

Menstruation is considered as 'impure'

Menstruation is still seen as filthy and impure on a cultural level in many regions of India. This myth's origins may be traced back to the Vedic era, and it is connected to Indra's killing of Vritra. Because women are said to have shared some of Indra's guilt, it is said in the Veda that the guilt of murdering a brahmana is said to manifest itself every month as menstruation.

Furthermore, it is against Hindu tradition for women to go on with their daily activities when they are menstruating. Before being permitted to re-join her family and resume her daily responsibilities, she must first be "purified." According to science, ovulation, followed by a failed attempt at conception, which results in endometrial artery bleeding, is the underlying cause of menstruation. Cycle preparation comes next. Therefore, there doesn't seem to be any support for the notion that menstruating women are "impure."

Many young women and girls have limitations in their everyday lives just because they are having their period. For urban females, the main limitation during menstruation is to avoid the "puja" chamber, but for rural girls, it is to even avoid the kitchen! Menstruation-related cultural norms and religious taboos are frequently made worse by historical connotations with bad spirits, humiliation, and embarrassment related to sexual reproduction.

Arguments for the prohibition of women

Permitting women entry would be disrespectful to the deity. It has been proposed that the deity Ayyappan ought to be acknowledged like a person, endowing him with the right to privacy under Article 21 of the Constitution. as it is considered an invasion of Ayyappan's privacy when women and girls of reproductive age visit him without his consent.

Only societal reforms are covered by Clause (2) of Article 25 of the Indian Constitution, as religious matters are covered by Article 26 of the Constitution. Clause (2) of Article 25 of the Indian Constitution guarantees access to public Hindu religious institutions to all classes and sections of society. Under Article 26(b), every religious organisation has the right to administer its own religious affairs.

In accordance with Rule 3(b) of the Kerala Hindu Places of Public Worship (Authorization of Entry) Rules, 1965, women are not permitted on the grounds of the Sabarimala temple. In Riju Prasad Sarma v. State of Assam, the Guwahati High Court held that religious traditions protected by Articles 25 and 26 are impervious to challenge under other sections of Part III of the constitution.

Religious Theories

1. Naishtika Brahmacharya:

According to Hindu tradition, a man's life is split into four stages: the brahmacharya (celibate student), the grihastha (married householder), the vanaprastha (woodland dweller), and the sannyasa (religious renunciate). A young boy is supposed to spend his time studying holy Hindu books under the loving direction of his guru during the 25 years that make up Brahmacharya.

According to tradition, a young man's Brahmacharya phase ends at the age of 25 and is replaced by the Grihastha phase. However, the Brahmachari has the option to renounce Grihastha and pursue a life of asceticism in order to achieve spiritual liberation; in this case, he must uphold celibacy and coexist in close proximity to his teacher.

Because of sensory disengagement, the Naishtika Brahmachari must only perform the bare minimum of tasks required for incorporeal revival. It is forbidden to deceive the five senses of sight, hearing, touch, smell, and taste. The senses shouldn't develop egotism or greed. If a Naishtika Brahmachari comes upon a feast of meat and wine, he must resist the impulse to indulge and instead look for basic sustenance.

Swami Ayyapa is also labelled as Naishtika Brahmachari.

2. Other Religious Theories:

Two explanations for why it was forbidden for menstruation women to enter the temple are:

According to a tale, Lord Ayyappa forbids menstruating women from entering the temple in remembrance of Malikapurathamma, a lady-demon who was vanquished by Ayyappa and then proposed to him. The Lord had stipulated that he would marry her the day pilgrims stopped coming to see him in Sabarimala. Some ladies decide not to go inside the temple because they feel that doing so would be disrespectful to Malikappurathamma's love and sacrifice.

The alternative mythology regards Lord Ayyappa as a historical hero who, after slaying an Arab invader by the name of Babar or Vavar, eschewed all earthly pleasures, including contact with women. He was born into the royal family of the kingdom located in Patthanamittha.

History

Since at least the 19th century, women of reproductive age have been prohibited from entering the Sabarimala temple, according to the Memoir of the Survey of the Travancore and Cochin States. Before 1991, when the Kerala High Court banned women from entering Sabarimala, a few of women had done so, mainly for religious purposes. There are accounts of female pilgrims going to the temple to hold their children's first rice-feeding ceremony or Chorounu, there. Even the Maharani of Thiruvithamkoor stopped at the shrine on May 13, 1940. The Devaswom Board, which looks after the temple and its grounds, was also fined Rs. 7,500 for allowing the filmmaker to shoot a movie at Sabarimala. Young actors Jayashree, Sudha Chandran, Anu, Vadivukkarasi, and Manorama were fined Rs. 1000 apiece in 1986 for dancing close to the god at the pathinettam padi (18 steps) for the Tamil film Nambinar Keduvathillai. Also claiming to have entered Sabarimala and touched the idol in 1986, when she was a young lady, is former Karnataka politician Jayamala.

In 1990, a ceremony in Sabarimala was organised when the granddaughter of a former Devaswom commissioner was fed rice in front of female relatives. After a legal lawsuit over this incident, the high court of Kerala forbade women and girls between the ages of 10 and 50 from visiting Sabarimala.

The district collector Valsala Kumari, 42, visited the Sabarimala shrine in 1995 with special permission, but she did not ascend the pathinettam padi, or 18 stairs, to the inner sanctuary. She wanted to acquire firsthand information about the circumstances at the temple for the purposes of her official responsibilities. She became the first woman to be accepted as genuine by the temple's officials as a result. The local news stated that two young women who may have been the spouses of VIPs had entered the temple despite police supervision the same year. The Sabarimala temple's administrators made it necessary for female visitors to provide identification verifying their age in January 2018.

A petition was filed by S. Mahendran in 1990 based on the claim that young ladies were travelling to Sabarimala. Justices K. Paripoornan and K. Balanarayana Marar of the Kerala High Court issued the ruling in 1991, banning women and girls between the ages of 10 and 50 from visiting Sabarimala. They claimed that this limitation was required by custom. The High Court also instructed Kerala's government to use police force, if required, to bar women from accessing the shrine.

The final judgement by the high court was that, the Devaswom Board's restrictions on women do not contravene Articles 15, 25, or 26 of the Indian Constitution. This restriction is also not in violation of the provisions of the Hindu Place of Public Worship (Authorization of Entry) Act, 1965, as there is no restriction on entry to a temple for Hindus of different sections or classes, whereas the prohibition only applies to women in a specific age group and not to all women.

Provisions in favour of entry of women

1. Article 14 in The Constitution Of India 1949

Equality before law The State shall not deny to any person equality before the law or the equal protection of the laws within the territory of India Prohibition of discrimination on grounds of religion, race, caste, sex or place of birth.

2. Article 15(1) in The Constitution Of India 1949

The State shall not discriminate against any citizen on grounds only of religion, race, caste, sex, place of birth or any of them

3. Article 17 of the Indian constitution talks about abolition of untouchability:

In the Sabarimala Temple case, Justice Chandrachud had ruled that untouchability extends beyond caste-related inequities to include some types of gender discrimination, and that excluding women and labelling them as impure owing to menstruation is a form of untouchability. Women may be subject to age-based restrictions (between 10 and 50) for the remainder of their lives as a person's lifespan is not guaranteed to reach 50–55 years.

Neither the Act nor the Constitution define untouchability. It alludes to a societal custom that discriminates against members of particular oppressed classes purely on the basis of their place of origin. Others were thought to be contaminated by their bodily contact. The so-called untouchable classes were forbidden from using the same wells as the higher castes or the ponds or tanks they used. They experienced several limitations and were forbidden from entering some temples. Untouchability in Indian society can refer to a variety of types of prejudice that go beyond caste.

4. Article 21 in The Constitution Of India 1949

Protection of life and personal liberty No person shall be deprived of his life or personal liberty except according to procedure established by law

5. Article 25 in The Constitution Of India 1949

Freedom of conscience and free profession, practice and propagation of religion. Subject to public order, morality and health and to the other provisions of this Part, all persons are equally entitled to freedom of conscience and the right freely to profess, practise and propagate religion

The Protection of Civil Rights Act, 1955

As stated in Article 17 of the Constitution, "Civil Rights" are defined as "any rights accruing to a person as a result of the eradication of untouchability". All offences covered by the Act are no longer subject to compounding. According to the law, it is illegal to keep someone from entering a place of public worship or from engaging in religious activity, or to bar them from entering a store, a restaurant open to the public, a hotel, or a place of public entertainment. It is also illegal to keep someone from receiving goods or services from a business or to refuse to admit them to a hospital. Additionally, it is illegal to preach untouchability, practise it, or defend it on the basis of religious, philosophical, historical, or other justifications while insulting a member of a Scheduled Caste.

Discrimination against women based on biological characteristics that are distinct to the female gender is prohibited by the Constitution's Articles 14 (equality), 15 (discrimination abolition), and 17 (abolition of untouchability), and is also prohibited by Article 51A of the Directive Principles of State Policy (DPSP) (e).

The temple's trust gets its funds from the Consolidated Fund. Thus, the temple is a public place of worship and not a private property. Menstruation is a biological phenomenon of ovulation. There doesn't appear to be any justification for the myth that menstruating women are "impure," therefore. One's dignity and religion are intrinsically linked as a way of life. When one gender is marginalised in favour of another, one's fundamental freedom to practise and profess one's faith is compromised.

Supreme court precedents

The decision to eliminate the restriction on women visiting the Sabarimala shrine was made by the bench's four judges ; Hon'ble Chief Justice of India Dipak Misra, Justice R F Nariman, Justice A M Khanwilkar, Justice D Y Chandrachud and Justice Indu Malhotra. The 5-Judge Bench of the Supreme Court rendered its decision in the Sabarimala Temple Entry controversy on September 28, 2018. A 4:1 majority ruled that it is unlawful for the temple to exclude women. It was decided that the practise infringed the female worshippers' basic right to freedom of religion (Article 25(1)). The Kerala Hindu Places of Public Worship Rules, 1965, which permitted the exclusion of women based on tradition, were declared unlawful by the Bench.

Speaking for himself and Khanwilkar J, CJI Dipak Misra noted that religion is a way of life that is inextricably related to one's dignity. The basic right to practise and proclaim one's religion is violated when one gender is excluded in favour of another. He claimed that the Sabarimala Temple's practise of excluding women between the ages of 10 and 50 years deprived women of their right to the freedom of religion protected by Article 25.(1). Furthermore, it was ruled that Lord Ayyappa's followers had not met the constitutional requirements to be recognized as a separate religious group. It was decided that if the Ayyappans identify as Hindus, the exclusion of women cannot be considered a fundamental aspect of their religion.

The State's duty for social change under Article 25(2) overrode the temple's denominational right to govern its own internal affairs under Article 26(b) (b). According to Article 25(2)(b), the State may pass legislation to change Hindu denominations. It permits the State to pass any law that admits all "classes and sections" of Hindus to a public Hindu institution. Women were included in the gendered category of "classes and sections" according to Justice Misra. Only Justice Indu Malhotra, in the Supreme Court's five-judge Constitutional bench headed by Chief Justice of India Deepak Mishra, did not oppose women's admittance restrictions and instead delivered a dissenting opinion. She maintained that a "harmonization" of many conflicting claims to fundamental rights is necessary for constitutional morality in a secular society like India. Regardless matter how reasonable or sensible a religious denomination's traditions are, the court, according to her, must accept their freedom to regulate their own affairs.

Conclusion

Where there is a breach of a fundamental right, we must focus on constitutional morality. Documentary information is the only way to determine if a practise is fundamentally important to a religion or not. Religious freedoms are crucial components for a democracy's efficient working. All people are guaranteed equality under the Indian Constitution. Societal patriarchy should not be granted the authority to restrict a citizen's right to pray. There should be equality for all.

CHAPTER XI

Tibet's fall between two stools

Written by Bhavya Shridhar (2nd Semester, BA. LL.B - Chandigarh University, Mohali).

Introduction

Tibet is a region on the Tibetan Plateau in Asia, spanning about 2.4 million km2 – nearly a quarter of China's territory. It is the traditional homeland of the Tibetan people as well as some other ethnic groups. Tibet has been considered a part of china for a very long period. As its culture and Buddhism are part of Chinese culture. But now there's been a conflict going on between the two as Tibet wishes to be autonomous. They want to prevent Tibetan culture, religion and language from being eroded to the point of extension whereas china wants full control over Tibet in order to develop better facilities so that it can attain economical benefits to bring better stability in the region. The nature of Tibet's relationship with China in the intervening period is a matter of debate.

The root of the conflict between China and Tibet

The China-Tibet conflict is now in its eighth decade and the historical relationship between the two is at the core of the conflict. This conflict is often viewed as an religious conflict. It is generally believed that China and Tibet were independent prior to the Yuan dynasty although the People's Republic of China asserts that Tibet has been a part of China since the Mongol-led Yuan dynasty. The Republic of China (ROC) asserted that "Tibet was placed under the sovereignty. of China" when the Qing dynasty (1636–1912) ended the brief Nepalese invasion. All these claims brought a chaos between the two. In 1949 Mao Zedong proclaims the founding of the People's Republic of China (PRC), a communist state born out of a brutal and bloody civil war. Zedong threatens Tibet with "liberation". Immediately after china's freedom in 1949 they starting threating the sovereignty of the Tibet. The Chinese waged a border war with Tibet while formally urging Tibet to join the Chinese Republic, claiming all along to the world that Tibet already was one of China's 'five races'. In 1950 The Dalai Lama, who is also regarded as the spiritual leader and as a living God, officially becomes head of state. Soon china had invaded Tibet, defeated its army, and established control over large parts of Tibetan territories. Later China forced Tibet to sign a treaty in 1951 which was known as 17 points. "Agreement on Measures for the Peaceful Liberation of Tibet". The alternative, the occupying forces said, was an immediate military operation in the remaining parts of Tibet. The "agreement" reflected the Chinese government's recognition of Tibet's unique and distinct historical, political, and cultural status in relation to the PRC at that time. Tibetans opposed this "agreement" as nothing less than a death warrant of their centuries-old history of independence. They were particularly indignant with the circumstances under which their delegates had been forced to sign it. In fact, Tibetan Prime Minister clearly told Chinese Representative that the Tibetan "people did not accept the agreement". Though the Chinese claim the agreement was mutual and cordial, and though the Tibetans at the time signed it, the Tibetan government-in-exile later claimed that it was signed under duress.

This treaty didn't stop China from governing Tibet, they soon started introducing communist Chinese policies and increased troops in the region. The Chinese violated the following points. The Tibetan people have the rights to exercise national regional autonomy under the unified leadership of the Central People's Government. The central authorities also will not alter the established status, functions and powers of the Dalai Lama. Officials of various ranks shall hold office as usual. The religious beliefs, customs and habits of the Tibetan people shall be respected, and lama monasteries shall be protected.

The local government of Tibet should carry out reforms of its own accord. The communist reforms were introduced in Kham and Amado [regions of Tibet] against the wishes of the Tibetan people, the Tibetan way of life was forcibly changed and hundreds of Tibetan religious and cultural institutions were razed to the ground. The Tibetans reacted by taking up arms against the Chinese. Thousands of Tibetans died, many went to jail and were never seen again. The resistance gradually spread to central Tibet, culminating in the national uprising in Lhasa on March 10, 1959, and the escape of the Dalai Lama to India. On 29 April 1959, the Dalai Lama established the independent Tibetan government in exile in North India Dharamshala, where he resides.

India's perspective

India plays a very significant role in this conflict as we have given asylum to Dalai lama and his followers in Dharamshala, Himachal Pradesh. India's relations with Tibet developed when China was ready to impose war on Tibet. The Government of India, soon after India's independence, treated Tibet as a de facto independent country. The former Prime Minster Jawaharlal Nehru received a letter from the Tibetan leader claiming his boundary back. Nehru gave asylum to him in order to preserve the security and integrity of India and also because he was for the Tibetan refugees. The Government of India in 1960 provided some land to these refugees in Mysore during the initial days. Later many other Indian states were willingly providing lands for the settlement of Tibetan in exile. Even though this sympathetic act of India of criticized by China , many other foreign countries praise India. India not only provided funds for both education and heath which made Tibetan's in exile feel welcomed but also allowed political and religious freedoms of the Buddhists. Tibetan even organized a 'Tibetan government-in-exile 'which was appreciated by the Indian Government.

UN's stand on Tibet

A statement published by the UN in 2008 states that nor Tibet has been mentioned in the list of countries to be decolonized neither china in the administrating powers. Tibet has always been recognized as a part of China. United Nations General assembly has passed many resolutions urging to respect the rights of Tibetans and allowing them to live peacefully in their homeland. A resolution in 1961 calls for that "principle of self-determination of peoples and nations" applies to the Tibetan people. UN holds a lot of power when it comes to the conflict between two countries if UN takes a stand against China to vacate Tibet and let them have a peaceful spiritual Tibetan monarchy.

Conclusion

This Conflict between Tibet And China is a never-ending debate and will always be in controversial. The primary sources of conflict in Tibet are history and geography; Chinese security and sovereignty concerns; and the policies of the Chinese government in Tibet. While they bring attention to ethnic and religious differences between Tibetans and Chinese, these factors are what really drive the conflict in Tibet. As neither of them is willing to compromise anything in order to live there life peacefully. China is adamant that he wants to rule over Tibet and wants full control over the boarders as it sees it as a opportunity through which it can gradually capture all the other neighboring countries in order to be the most powerful country in the world. Tibet never had any boundary problems with either India, China, Nepal, Bhutan or any adjoining countries. China which had no boundary with most of these countries is trying to create boundary problems through Tibet and unnecessarily creating tension with not only India but with most of the countries. Dalai lama's going back to this homeland can create a lot of chaos not only to the Tibetans but also to the world. Its for the best that Tibetans should have there asylum in India for rest of there lives and preach the world about their customs, and develop more monasteries to prevent there religion from extinction. The other alternative that Tibetans hold is to share power and divide it between two, they can also that outside interference in order to settle the dispute, can also reconciliation which is of course easier to say than done. China to can set a better government in Tibet

CHAPTER XII

Marital rape: Need for criminalisation or not?

Written by Ramanpreet Singh Malhotra (2nd Semester, BA. LL.B - Chandigarh University, Mohali).

Introduction

Forcefully or by manipulating someone in unwanted sexual intercourse is regarded as 'rape'. Irrespective of the fact that the person is someone you are dating or married to. It is assumed that individuals tied in matrimonial or romantic relationships surrender their consent for sexual intercourse in doing so. However, it is to be taken into note that if either of the persons is not willing to give in their consent for the sexual activity, the decision is to be valued and should be left at it. Even so, if the partner indulges the other by force, threat, physical dominance or manipulation it is to be considered a sexual assault.

Spousal rape and intimate sexual violence may lead to or can be rightfully associated with Domestic Violence. Wherein, the victim has to go through occasional or constant abuse in terms of physical and mental aspects.

Statistical brief and its effects

Marital rape or intimate sexual abuse is more common than it seems to our eyes. A person might be witnessing and going through it and yet believing and justifying the abuse as a duty to be fulfilled in order to satisfy the needs of the partner in a relationship. According to the most recent National Family Health Survey (NFHS-5), nearly 1 in 3 Indian women falling under the age of 18 –49 have suffered some form of marital abuse and around 6% have experienced sexual violence. The NFHS-5 survey (2019-2021) was conducted in around 6.37 lakh sample households in707 districts in 28 states and 8 of the Union Territories, covering 7,24,115 women and 1,01,839 men to provide dis-aggregated estimates up to district level.

The survey said that 32% of ever-wedded ladies have experienced spousal physical, sexual, or emotional brutality, and 27% have endured at least one type of viciousness in the year preceding the survey. 29% of ever-hitched ladies have experienced spousal actual viciousness and 14%have experienced emotional brutality.

The adversity is such that the surviving person of sexual assault has a big impact on his/her perception and might not accept or see the things as the same before. Worldly relationships, sex and love do not hold the value to it once the person suffers the brutality, hiddenly associated with it. Sexual abuse or spousal rape may very much result in the desecration of one's mental peace and mental health. Moreover, physical sufferings are no less painful and they might take a long span of time to recover as well.

According to the psychological perspective, the very image of one's self is extremely influenced and affected. It leads to anxiety with context to sexual intercourse and intimacy of the partner. Likely in cases, it triggers the mental illness which demands the attention of medical treatment and psychiatric observations such as panic attacks, neurosis, depression, post traumatic disorder (PTSD).

A number of studies have shown that the effects on the mentality of marital rape victims are, in some cases so severe that they can reach a stage where they consider themselves as the guilty body for the violent behaviour and abuse of their partner. Considering them own as the cause of the inhumane behaviour of their spouse, the cause of their misfortune and the verbal insults thrown by the partner all the more amplifies their guilt.

It's lawful treatment in India

Marital rape is not an offense in India. Enactments in regards to marital rape in India are either non-existent or esoteric and dependant on the understanding by Courts. Section 375, the provision of rape in the Indian Penal Code (IPC), mentions as its exception clause- "Sexual intercourse by man with his own wife, the wife not being under 15 years of age, is not rape." As per section 376 of IPC, which provides punishment for rape, the rapist ought to be rebuffed with detainment of either portrayal for a term which might not be under 7 years but rather which may stretch out to life or for a term reaching out up to 10 years and should likewise be at risk to fine unless the lady raped is his own particular spouse, and is not under 12 years old, in which case, he might be rebuffed with detainment of either depiction for a term which may reach out to 2 years with fine or with both.

Hence marital rape is viewed as a rape just if the spouse is under 15 years old, and the seriousness of punishment is milder. There is no lawful security agreed to the spouse after the age of 15, which is against human rights directions. A similar law that accommodate the lawful period of agree for marriage to be 18, shields from sexual mishandle just those up to the age of 15. According to the Indian Penal Code, the cases wherein the spouse can be criminally arraigned for an offense of marital rape are as under:

When the wife is between 12 – 15 years of age, offence punishable with imprisonment upto 2 years or fine, or both; When the spouse is underneath 12 years old, offense culpable with detainment of either portrayal for a term which might not be under 7 years but rather which may reach out to life or for a term stretching out up to 10 years and should likewise be subject to fine; Rape of a judicially isolated spouse, offense culpable with detainment upto 2 years and fine; Rape of wife of above 15 years in age is not punishable.

Conclusion

With regards to the prior context, it can be rightfully concluded that treatment of Marital Rape is dealt with mild prosecution and not-so-severe penalty. As per my views, new policies should be formulated and put into action so as to protect the victims and rightfully deliver them the justice thus needed. Marital rape and sexual assault should be categorised into Criminal Offence and a legitimate procedure should be established to punish the abuser. Moreover, campaigns and awareness programmes should be organised and conducted by the Government in order to spread awareness about the 'Right to consent' in a sexual intercourse, vested within the hands of each person , aside from the fact that they share a marital relationship or not. Until and unless it is made clear and fed up into the minds of the coming as well as the existing generations that forcefully submitting your partner into a sexual intercourse without their consent is a crime, many more might become the victim of sexual abuse without even realising it.

CHAPTER XIII

China-India conflict and its implications at the geopolitical level

Written by Anisha Gupta (4th Semester, BA. LL.B - Chandigarh University, Mohali).

Introduction

India and China are still at an impasse in Eastern Ladakh, where Chinese territory lies across the Line of Actual Control. Modi might not have gone in person to the BRICS Summit because China refused to back out. Not only that, but India and China have been unable to agree on a time and place for the 16th round of discussions since the 15th round of corps commander-level talks in March. Since the two sides still differ on the most crucial issues, military and diplomatic talks have made little progress.

Recent Tawang Standoff

Things are getting worse between India and China. Along their disputed border in the Himalayas, the two world powers are fighting each other. The main cause is a disputed border that runs for 3,440 km (2,100 miles). Along the border, rivers, lakes, and snowcaps can cause the line to move. This can bring soldiers face to face and cause a fight.

Along the border, which is also called the Line of Actual Control, the two countries are also competing to build infrastructure. The fact that India is building a new road to a high-altitude air base is seen as one of the main reasons why Chinese troops will fight back in 2020.

Even though military leaders are talking, tensions remain. In December 2022, it had been more than a year since soldiers fought each other. It happened near the Tawang area of the Indian state of Arunachal Pradesh, which is in the far east of the country. A few soldiers got small injuries. Since a big fight in June 2020, there has been work to calm things down. The Galwan Valley battle, which was fought with sticks and clubs instead of guns, was the first time since 1975 that someone died in a fight between the two sides. At least 20 soldiers from India and 4 soldiers from China died.

China said that India had shot at its troops in September 2021. China was blamed by India for shooting into the air. If it's true, it would be the first time shots were fired at the border in 45 years. A deal made in 1996 said that guns and explosives couldn't be used near the border. In the same month, both countries agreed to leave a border area in the western Himalayas that they had been fighting over. In January 2021, there was another fight, and troops on both sides were hurt. It took place between Bhutan and Nepal, near the Indian state of Sikkim.

The latest fights between the Indian and Chinese armies in Arunachal Pradesh have shown once again how big of a problem China is for India. India and China have been in a standoff at the Ladakh border since April 2020. India's deployments in Eastern Ladakh have been the same as China's, and it has tried to stop the Chinese People's Liberation Army (PLA) from cutting into Indian territory.

Many analysts have talked about the recent Indo-US military exercises near the China border in Uttarakhand when writing about the fights in Arunachal Pradesh. Also, the latest report from the US Department of Defense says that China told the US that it shouldn't get in the way of its relationship with India. But the standoff in Ladakh hasn't been solved yet, and the PLA's strong stance in Arunachal Pradesh is likely also meant to send a political message. Also, it was interesting how the fight came about.

Geopolitical Implications

Aside from China's obvious interest in the strategically important state of Arunachal Pradesh, which it sees as Southern Tibet and claims in its entirety, there have been three major events that are important to know about to understand the political situation. First, the Chinese Communist Party held its party congress in October, and now Xi Jinping is in charge. He now has a stronger hold on the party, the military, and the government, and he is even more sure of his ability to show power abroad.

Second, since the G20 summit in Indonesia in November, the US and China have been trying to get back together and work out their differences. Because of this, China and Xi Jinping were in a much better position. Third, India became the rotating leader of the G20 on December 1. The Indian government wants to use the G20 summit and related meetings as a chance to show the world how far India has come on the world stage. In this case, it's important to understand the three main political messages behind the border fight with India.

The third and final point is to show strength and power in the neighbourhood. China's message is that if India, its biggest neighbour and a major power in Asia, could be pushed around in this way, then other weaker neighbours should get the point. They should be careful not to hurt China's feelings and not support Taiwan. Also, there could be a fourth, maybe less important reason: to take people's minds off the protests at home. China was in the middle of protests against the strict Covid-19 rules when the fights broke out.

By making things worse at the border in Arunachal Pradesh, China may have sent India a strong political message in addition to the obvious military effects. India needs to come up with a number of ways to stand up to China in a very important year.

India-China Galwan Standoff

The current state of relations between India and China is their lowest ever recorded. When compared to the Doklam standoff in 1967, which lasted 72 days, the current Galwan border conflict pales in comparison. Due to this, the first Indian life has been lost at the border in 45 years. Because of this, tensions between the two countries have escalated. It's clear that the assertive agenda pursued by Chinese President Xi Jinping stands in stark contrast to Deng Xiaoping's "low profile" foreign policy. Due to the lack of a clearly demarcated Line of Actual Control (LAC), border conflicts frequently arise between India and China. Numerous fights and other wrongdoings have taken place. In this episode, fighting broke out simultaneously in four different locations in Sikkim: the Galwan sector (which had never been an issue before), Demchok, Pangong lake, and Nathu-La. There were casualties on both sides, and it's unclear who provoked the fighting. In January 2021, satellite pictures showed that China built a new village about 2 km into the state of Arunachal Pradesh on the Indian side of the LAC. China has never recognised Arunachal Pradesh, but they say it is part of their country.

Reason for Increase In Chinese Aggression

There has been a lot of talk about why China is becoming more aggressive on the border:

a) The fact that India got rid of Article 370, which changed Ladakh's status,

b) A better relationship between the United States and India, or

c) The fact that relations between India and Taiwan are getting better.

Chinese Reaction Against Indian Geopolitics

China has tried to put India in its place because it is a stronger military power. Also, whenever there is a problem at home, China acts "risky" at the border to make people forget about their problems. In this episode, the Chinese government was criticised for how it dealt with the coronavirus pandemic.

China has asked that boundary disputes be kept separate from business matters. However, New Delhi has made it clear that things will not get back to normal between the two countries until the boundary is put back to how it was before. For example, India has banned fifty-nine popular Chinese apps like PubG, TikTok, and Shein as a way of getting back at China. Also, the Indian government has called for "atma nirbharta" to make the country less dependent on China (self-reliance). The Minister of Road Transport, Highways, and Micro, Small, and Medium Enterprises (MSME) also said that China's investments should be "discouraged" to show that even though India is weak militarily, it can hurt China economically. India's relationships with Australia, Japan, Indonesia, Vietnam, France, and the UK have all gotten better because of the standoff.

The two countries are rivals, thus China has gotten closer to India's foe, Pakistan, to exert pressure on India in exchange. The China-Pakistan Economic Corridor (CPEC) passes through Gilgit-Baltistan, which is located in Pakistan-administered Kashmir. There has been tension between the two countries over this issue since 1947. Any CPEC work done by China is now legitimate thanks to Pakistan's recent grant of "provincial status" to the region. Furthermore, China is getting engaged in Nepal's diplomatic problem just when relations between India and Nepal are at an all-time low. China's Belt and Road Initiative has resulted in billions of dollars in investments in Nepal (BRI). Another aspect of China's "debt trap diplomacy" involves a $1 billion loan to Sri Lanka. By taking these actions, China is seeking to pressure the Indian government from the outside.

India's Stern Action

There is hope that India can use coercive diplomacy to find a way to be defensive and still get what she wants. The border dispute between the two most powerful countries in South Asia is a very important issue that people all over the world are paying attention to. China may have become more important in South Asian politics, but India has made new diplomatic connections all over the world because of the tension. India has been asked to be a "guest country" at the G-7 summit, which China is not a part of. There is hope that India and China can come to an agreement through diplomatic means so that there are no more border disputes in the future.

India and China's fights at the border in Arunachal Pradesh have made things worse between the two countries at a time when India has just taken over the presidency of the G-20 and is planning around 200 meetings in more than 50 Indian cities leading up to the big summit in September 2023. China's presence at these events will be very important, so India's response to China's recent aggression, while firm, is also carefully worded so that it doesn't hurt India's G-20 presidency.

During the G-20 summit that took place this year in Indonesia, India played a very positive and important role in bringing people together and getting them to agree on the "Bali Declaration." Michael Kugelman has said that the world is more divided than it has ever been, and that multilateral forums are being dragged into bilateral wars. But India could also use this as a chance to show the world what kind of aggression it has been facing for decades.

China's recent border attacks could lead India to use its G-20 presidency to bring this issue to the attention of the world. Even though most of what's on the G-20 agenda is economic, China won't be able to use this as an excuse to skip or disrupt meetings because it wants to win back the world's trust after the zero-Covid problems.

Also, the US, which put sanctions on China over semiconductors for reasons of national security, has a position that is closer to that of India. Even though China recently challenged US sanctions at the WTO, it might not find many people who are willing to separate geopolitics and economics. At the G-20, which is more of an economic forum, India and China have more similar interests than different ones. This means that anything China did to hurt India would hurt its own national interests.

Analysis of India-U.S. relations applying the China test

Relations are more based on interests: New Delhi's relationship with Washington has been complicated, but it is becoming more normal and based on interests. Washington wants to get involved in southern Asia again, even though it has left the area (Pakistan, South Asia in general, the Indo-Pacific, and perhaps even the Taliban).

India's growing proximity to the U.S.: It seems that one of the lessons New Delhi learned from the standoff with China along the Line of Actual Control in 2020 was that it may have been a result of India's growing proximity to the U.S. Strategic cooperation between India and the U.S. in the area could help China: Since Beijing wants to control the area, it is clear that it is not in its best interest for the U.S. to get involved in the area again or for India and the U.S. to get closer. If so, the lack of or lukewarm strategic engagement between India and the U.S. in the region is exactly what would help Beijing reach its long-term goals.

Conclusion

Since the standoff in Ladakh began 32 months ago, India's relationship with China has gone from bad to worse, and it doesn't look like it will get better unless Beijing makes a big change in how it sees India and the region. The Indian foreign minister, S. Jaishankar, said this about the state of the relationship: "The state of the border will determine the state of the relationship. Delhi's leadership of the G20 may open up ways to work with Beijing, but the country needs a clear vision and a grand strategy to deal with the China challenge before it can do that.

China says it wants to reset relations, but its words and actions don't always match up. This makes it less likely that other countries, like India, will take China's words seriously.

Delhi should try to get talks on the diplomatic level going at the same time that it is getting its military ready. No matter what is happening on the ground or how things will get worse, the government should talk to the Opposition parties as soon as possible. When there are problems at the borders, the country needs a lot of politicians to agree on what to do. a

CHAPTER XIV

A critical analysis of Niqah Halala in Islam

Written by Jiya Grover (2nd Semester, BA. LL.B - Chandigarh University, Mohali).

Abstract

It looks at the social evil prevailing in every society .these days, where the religious framework is changed by the monopolizers of the religion as per their will. as niqah halala is a concept in Islam for the discouragement of divorce but has been interpreted wrongly and just made as an economical work for some local clerics and the women have been made a game of prey by the men.

Keywords: divorce, halala, social evil, monopolizers, victim, taheel.

Introduction

Taheel marriage commonly or famously known as niqah halala it is a form of marriage to marry the divorced husband again, in this basically if a husband divorces his wife the three times without maintaining any type of sexual relationship with her in the period of the that's basically three mensuration cycles. Divorce is considered to be done according to the Islam.

Holy books in Islam don't state anything such as nikah halala in its religious practices what it states is just about niqah people these days have interpreted it wrongly acc. To their requirements. Husbands these days arbitrarily grants divorce to his wife without even a second opinion and then at the time of realizing it, forces her to perform niqah halala which is totally defined as shamed marriage or unlawful according to the holy texts in Islam. What actually it defines is that, that niqah halala is not a contract based marriage but is that she is free from that matrimonial bond and is now an independent women who can choose to do anything according to her will. The concept was chiefly made to make man realize his mistake for leaving his wife as a punishment to him

Niqah halala as a religiously sectioned rape

Generation of men and women had grown up with an ideology of that marriage ends with the pronouncements of the word talaq and can only revived after the ritual or the practice of halala, but this practice of instant divorce and instant marriage is not only a unjust to women but also a thinking of men who uses the grab of piety to satisfy their thrust of variety of women in their bed. The idea practice of halala is more prevalent only in the Indian subcontinent.

Which has a sizeable population of indo-pak origin. It is almost impossible to find a man for women who will marry her for just giving her divorce, in that cases the local clerics make a contract of marrying a women and then divorcing her after few days after making physical relations with her, this has become a market in which the women is actually used by the clerics in the veil of halala. Due to the loose of temperament and unjustified pronouncement of talaq, creates an unjust and a victimized situation for the women.

Women as an unfortunate victim

Where women is considered as a back bone to family the one who serves food and sacrifices everything for them and we as a mean society is asking for a very huge sacrifice of her dignity in the cover of a religious traditions i.e niqah halala where even the tradition was made to discourage the divorce and to punish the husband who has given divorce to her without valuing her efforts. the women is being used as a tool which directly violates her right to dignity under article 14,15 of indian constitution . they are forced to do halala with their brother in law ,father in law just for remarrying her former husband without her consent , she is forced to maintain the sexual relation with the unknown man .in many cases there are the contracts which says that the man will marry her and after maintain the sexual relations with her will divorce her the next day or after few days all this contract also costs a monetary value.and most of the times these contract based halala practices are encouraged by the local Maulvis. This a very brutal side of halala where firstly she is forced to do halala and even after the contract the man refuses to divorce her and abuses her sexually as well as mentally after using her neither her former husband nor the contracted person accepts her making her a prey of the game, even the society rejects her and her personal identity is totally destroyed.

Actually the concept of halala in Islam was made to discourage the practice of divorce. We should understand these interpretations which are prevailing in the society and making women a unfortunate victim. Halala as a practice not only that destroys women emotionally and physically but also interpreted in a way which gives the youth and the generations a message that women can be taken for granted. Every practice has its own pros and cons.

Conclusion

All the religions make the framework of their respective religion in a way that it gives a good deeds and intentions .this is only some interpreters that interprets the religious framework as per their will and completely changes the meaning and sole idea of that frame work which is for the betterment of the society.

As halala has been described by the prophet of Islam in quran in surah-al-baqarah in verse 229 of chapter2 that this religious practice is practiced to make a man realize of his mistake of giving her wife a divorce by losing temperament. All what it states was that the halala can be practiced if she in future after marrying anyone else wants to marry her former husband rather than any third party. Practice was not described what actually is being performed in the today's society and women are being sexually harassed and used and thrown out. Quran actually defines it as a shame marriage and a curse to a person who forcefully asks her or performs halala with her. Every religion gives teaching to respect women for the growth and betterment of family and society both, we just need to understand the religious practices clearly without any interpretations by the social contractors.

CHAPTER XV

Capital Punishment: A Bone of Contention

Written by Vishakha (2nd Semester, BA. LL.B - Chandigarh University, Mohali).

Abstract

Capital punishment, also known as death penalty, is a government-sanctioned practice whereby a person is put to death by the state as a punishment for a crime. Since at present 58 countries, including the USA, which is considered to be the lighthouse of the Western economic and human development, still retain it, although thousands of books and papers had already been written about this topic, it seemed, nevertheless, both morally and academically correct and useful to redact an analysis of this juridical phenomenon. Having read through a considerable amount of publications, we found out a major issue: the researches carried out in the past significantly lacked of a statistical base to lean on. We decided, than, to understand the cause of this lack and possibly to implement a more precise work, merging together the data to us available. Before discussing the subject in deeper detail, we decided to deal with a brief history of the capital punishment. The reader will certainly be surprised by the partiality and incompleteness of the work, but we believed this paper was not the place for a universal history of death penalty from the dawn of the human civilization. We opted for a methodological approach, which inquires the Occidental experience from the theoretical point of view. For reasons of shortness, we presented only the main thinkers and theories, but we are sure the benevolent read will excuse us.

Introduction

Capital punishment also known as death penalty, is a legal practice in India which a person is put to death by state for serious crimes. It is legal but rarely voted and also a highly debated mater in India. Execution is not always carried out, because of the possibility of commutation to life imprisonment. Since 1995 it has been used only five times on Auto Shankar in 1995, Dhananjoy Chatterjee in 2004, Ajmal Kasab in 2012, Afzal Guru in 2013 and Yakub Memon in 2015. It is better if death penalty doesn't take place in an ideal society there is nothing to debate on this. Gandhi ji gave his strong arguments that why capital punishment is immoral as he was the one who was against it. He said that there is no difference whether a person kills any person or any state kills any person. If chance you hang someone on death and later you come to know that he was innocent then the chances of improvement become zero. For example their can be a possibility that in a house a child commits a crime and their parents become worried about their detention then they try to take blame on themselves, in this case if death penalty is applied then an innocent become the prisoner and the chances of improvement becomes zero.

The another reason behind criminal is not that he has committed a crime but the reason are his situations, because his situation was wrong we cannot put him to death. in one sense it looks as we have used a person as a tool which is not good. One most famous personality who was against death penalty was Cesare Beccaria and with context of all his statements a day called world day against death penalty is celebrated on 10th October. All the above statements are against capital punishment. Above all these statements if you ask me personally I would say death penalty is a good arrangement for which our supreme court has said that it should be used in rarest of rare cases which include firstly, cases in which there is not even a single chance of suspection secondly, their should be less or no role of circumstances behind his crime thirdly, crime should be that much heinous that not giving death penalty for that crime becomes a crime in itself for someone. Looking at all the conditions if we give someone death penalty then its logical.

If we go deeply on this matter of providing capital punishment we will feel mercy as well as anger on them and if we not go deeply then we will have a feeling of hatred for them and a person who is only hating mean that he is not ready to go deep. Hating is an easy option but if you will go little deep you will understand that for increase in such crimes there are few social and economic conditions too which can be held responsible and then you will also feel there are many such cases happening in the society which are not even being noticed. Another thought that comes to our mind is that their might become chances of their improvement. Sometimes giving death penalty to someone acts as a ointment on country's wound.

In this situation if someone raises the question of human rights then I would say human rights are for the humans of the nation and for the demons there are and there should be demon rights. Though its arguable, in principle, we do agree that the guilty deserves to be punished. The degree and mode of punishment, for grave offences, is the bone of contention here. This raises two questions: One whether death penalty is in itself justified as a form of punishment or not. Second, if death penalty serves the purpose of punishment better than other forms, say life imprisonment.

Comparison to Saudi Arabia

Saudi Arabia did mass execution of 81 criminals, the largest execution in mass history of Saudi on 12th March 2022. In Saudi Arabia death penalty is a legal penalty which provides punishment for cases including murder, witchcraft, rape, adultery, terrorism. The executed convicts were said to be involved in terrorism and murder, they were members of Al-Qaida, ISIS and supporters of Houthi rebels. Under Sharia Law Saudi can impose death penalty under 3 categories i.e.

1. Hudud means imposing fixed punishments for specific crimes like apostasy, adultery and sodomy.

2. Qisas which includes eye-for-an-eye retaliatory punishment. This category mainly includes crimes like murder. Under Qisas the family of the victim can demand death penalty or pardon the convicts in exchange of blood money.

3. Tazir crimes included by national regulations like drug trafficking, theft, espionage etc. Use of beheading for execution and execution of for nationals has attracted criticism for Saudi.

Conclusion

Contemplating over capital punishment has been ramping on for a countless no. of years. It is true that the death sentence is not the solution to the increase in crimes but at the same time, capital punishment inflicts physiological fear in the minds of the people. In many countries, the use of this punishment has helped to deter crimes and change the minds of people against committing heinous crimes. Capital punishment should be given in the rare of the rarest cases after proper investigation of the criminal's offence.

CHAPTER XVI

Cyberstalking: A virtual reality

Written by Riya Sharma (2nd Semester, BA. LL.B - Chandigarh University, Mohali).

Abstract

Our society has come to rely on the sheer size, technological power, and Lightening fast speed of the Internet to seek out immeasurable pages of information, explore the unknown, and communicate with virtually anyone, anywhere, and at any time across the globe. The Internet has literally become a fertile breeding ground for an entirely new and unique type of criminal offender hereafter known as the cyber stalker. The phenomenon of stalking itself is as old as humankind itself. The past years and the expansion of digitalization have put the crime of stalking in a new light. Technology and tools available to curb it have many limitations and are not easy to implement. The continued widespread use of technology and the anonymous nature of cyberstalking will likely contribute to the continued increase in this type of crime.

This paper presents a glimpse into the current state of knowledge in cyber-stalking, Its impact and its jurisdiction in the world. The paper also gives a brief on the kinds of cyber-stalking.

Keywords: Cyberstalking, cyber-stalker, Digitalization.

Introduction: What is Cyberstalking

Privacy is dead and social media hold the smoking gun", said Peter Cashmore, founder of Mashable. The prolific growth of technology has engendered a plethora of next-generation media and communications platforms (e.g., Instagram, Facebook, Snapchat) that enable higher degrees of technology-supported interactions between individuals across the globe. Technology has provided stalkers with additional tools to electronically stalk and harass their victims and added new dimensions to the impact of this crime on victims. One of them is Cyberstalking.

Cyberstalking is the use of the Internet or other electronic means to stalk or harass an individual, group, or organization. It may include false accusations, defamation, slander and libel. It may also include monitoring, identity theft, threats, vandalism, solicitation for sex, doxing, or blackmail. It is not the mere annoyance of unsolicited e-mail. It is methodical, deliberate, and persistent. Unsolicited e-mail is one of the most common forms of harassment, including hate, obscene, or threatening mail.

Cyberstalkers use a variety of techniques. They may initially use the Internet to identify and track their victims. They may then send unsolicited e-mails, including hate, obscene or threatening mail. Live chat harassment abuses the victim directly or through electronic sabotage. The rapidly advancing technology also makes it possible for abusers to use Spyware which is computer software or possibly a hardware device that allows someone to monitor and get information about someone else's computer use. Fighting against the multifaceted issue of stalker-ware requires global and collective action from law enforcement, cybersecurity vendors, information technology security firms, non-governmental organizations, and academia. For this reason, several key actors in the global cybersecurity ecosystem have come together and created the Coalition Against stalker-ware to protect users against this malevolent software. The key goals of this coalition are twofold: focusing on improving the detection and mitigation of stalker-ware on the one hand and, on the other, raising broader awareness of the issue alongside organizations that work directly with victims and survivors.

Bocij, Griffiths and McFarlane. Defined cyber stalking as "a group of behaviour in which an individual, group of individuals or organization, uses information and communications technology to harass one or more individuals. Such behaviour may include, but are not limited to, the transmission of threats and false accusations, identity theft, data theft, damage to data or equipment, computer monitoring, the solicitation of minors for sexual purposes and confrontation"

The stalker can assume control of the victim's computer and the only defensive option for the victim is to disconnect and relinquish their current Internet address. The situation is like discovering that anytime you pick up the phone, a stalker is on-line and in control of your phone.

Kinds of Stalking

There are three kinds of cyber stalking:

1. Email-Stalking: Direct communication through email;
2. Internet Stalking: Global communication through internet;
3. Computer Stalking: Unauthorised control of another person's Computer.

E-mail stalking:

Unsolicited e-mail is one of the most common forms of harassment, including hate, obscene, or threatening mail. As a medium, Email incorporates the immediacy of a phone call and introduces the degree of separation entitled in a letter. Other forms of harassment include sending the victim viruses or high volume of electronic junk mail. It is important to note here that sending viruses or telemarketing solicitations alone do not constitute stalking.

Internet Stalking:

Here in this case stalkers can comprehensively use the Internet in order to slander and endanger their victims. Generally, cyber stalking is accompanied by traditional stalking behaviours such as threatening phone calls, vandalism of property, threatening mail, and physical attacks.

Computer Stalking: The third mode of cyber stalking is computer stalking which exploits the Workings of the Internet and the Windows operating system in order to assume control over the computer of the targeted victim. The stalker can communicate directly with their target as soon as the target computer connects in any way to the internet. Stalker hijack the IP addresses in order to follow the activities of the victim.

Webcam Hijacking:

Internet stalkers would attempt to trick you into downloading and putting in a malware-infected file that may grant them access to your webcam. the method is therefore sneaky that it's probably you wouldn't suspect anything strange.

Observing location check-ins on social media:

In case you're adding location check-ins to your Facebook posts, you're making it overly simple for an internet stalker to follow you by just looking through your social media profiles.

Catfishing:

Catfishing happens via social media sites, for example, Facebook, when internet stalkers make counterfeit user-profiles and approach their victims as a companion of a companion. Cyber-harassment can also involve the posting or other distribution of false information or rumours about an individual to damage the victim's social standing, interpersonal relationships, and/or reputation (i.e., a form of cyber-smearing). This false information is posted on websites, chat rooms, discussion forums, social media, and other online sites to damage the reputations of people and businesses.

Impact of cyberstalking

When it comes to the impact of stalking the high prevalence numbers are especially worrying given that this behaviour imposes a great strain on the private lives of the victims. Several studies have indicated that victims experience personality changes, suffer from insomnia and they often show symptoms of Post Traumatic Stress Disorder (PTSD) or other psychiatric and psychological complaints.10 Thirty percent of female victims and twenty percent of male victims sought psychological counselling and seven percent never returned to work as a result of the stalking.

Furthermore, the posting or otherwise distributing of false information on bulletin boards, chat-rooms or through direct e-mails, also known as 'cyber-smearing', can even be more harmful than equivalent behaviours in the offline world, since information on the internet is accessible to a large audience and it often remains accessible for a long period of time.

Jurisdiction of cyberstalking on an international level

One of the issues that always needs to be addressed in cases of cross-border crimes is the question of jurisdiction. Which country has the right to prosecute and convict suspects and, if more than one country has jurisdiction, which claim shall prevail?

The reasonableness standard suggests that the exercise of jurisdiction requires a close connection to the crime. Not every country uses the same standards for exercising jurisdiction, this can lead to two sorts of jurisdictional conflicts: negative and positive ones. A negative jurisdictional conflict arises when no particular country claims jurisdiction. The Positive jurisdiction occur when more than one jurisdiction claims jurisdiction over the one cyber-crime. One reason for not claiming jurisdiction may lie in the absence of domestic legislation that establishes jurisdiction over the conduct. Another reason to abstain from claiming jurisdiction could lie in the insignificance of the harm done to other countries or in the lack of means or the unwillingness to prosecute of the country in which the perpetrator resides principle of territoriality is usually understood to include the 'location of the act' only. Jurisdiction is based upon a person having been physically present within a country's territory at the time the offense was committed. If a country would hold on to the principle of territoriality, this could seriously hamper prosecution and conviction of international. The jurisdictional issues in relation to cyber-Stalking being tested in the courts.

While jurisdictional issues result in difficulties in investigating and prosecuting cyber-stalking, these problems are not specific to this only but occurs in other cyber-crimes also.

Suggestions and Conclusion

This paper has presented an overview of cyber-stalking as a form of stalking that takes advantage of the affordances of the electronic environment. The literature on cyber stalking is still in its infancy; however, the incidence of cyber stalking is expected to increase as the Internet becomes even more popular than it is today, especially amongst society's youth. There is a need to extend the boundaries of our perceptions of stalking to include current conceptions of cyber-stalking and future methods of stalking that may arise. The fast pace at which technology changes, as well as, the inexpensive cost of technologies make it easier for a person to track and stalk a victim. Studies based on victim experiences need to be explored in depth so that the appropriate laws are written to protect victims of cyberstalking. Everybody should be aware about these cybercrimes and should not share address, phone number or email id on social media, A collaborative effort from victims, law enforcement, and private and public sectors is needed in order to combat cyberstalking and develop an effective response to the problems.

References

P. Bocij, M.D Griffiths, &L. McFarlane, Cyber-stalking: A new challenge for criminal law, The new criminal lawyer 122(2002) , 3-5

https://www.academia.edu/69907470/Cyberstalking_a_new_challenge_for_criminal_law?from_sitemaps=true&version=2

L. Cox & B. Speziale, Survivors of stalking, their voices and lived experiences, Journal of women and social work 24 (2009) 5-10

https://journals.sagepub.com/doi/10.1177/0886109908326815

A Review of: "Cyberstalking: harassment in the internet age and How to protect your family

https://www.tandfonline.com/doi/abs/10.1080/01972240500253665?journalCode=utis20

Emma Ogilvie, Cyberstalking, Trends and issues in crime and criminal justice, Australian Institute of Criminology

https://www.aic.gov.au/sites/default/files/2020-05/tandi166.pdf

Joey L. Blanch and Wesley l.Hsu, cyber Misbehaviour, An introduction to violent crime on the internet, (May 2016)Volume 64, 2-11

https://www.justice.gov/usao/file/851856/download

Lynne Robert, Jurisdictional and Definitional concerns with computer-mediated and interpersonal crimes: An analysis on Cyberstalking, International Journal of cyber criminology

https://www.cybercrimejournal.com/pdf/lynnerobertsijccjan2008.pdf

Interpol, https://www.interpol.int/en/Crimes/Cybercrime

United Nations Office on Drugs and Crime, Interpersonal cybercrime, Cyber stalking and cyber harassment, Module 12

https://www.unodc.org/e4j/zh/cybercrime/module-12/key-issues/cyberstalking-and-cyberharassment.html

F. Mishna, Michael Saini and Steven Solomon, ongoing and online: Children and Youth's Preceptions of cyberbullying, children and youth service review 31(12) 1222- 1228, (2009).

CHAPTER XVII

Relevance of South China Sea globally

Written by Sonu Jangid (4th Semester, LL.B - Chandigarh University, Mohali).

Abstract

The territorial and maritime conflicts in the South China Sea are often considered as "intractable," and collaborative development of marine regions susceptible to overlapping jurisdictional claims is sometimes proposed as a viable path forward. The investigation is predicated on the viewpoint that the states that are asserting their sovereignty claim sovereignty over the islands in the South China Sea (the Claimants) will be unable to do so. For the foreseeable future, the geographical sovereignty conflicts should be resolved via dialogue. It is also taken into account that they might not be keen to disclose their information agreement to have the territorial issues heard by either an international court or an arbitral panel court or tribunal, then request that court / tribunal to decide which nation has the superior case. A pretension to national sovereignty as a direct consequence of this, we have not made any effort to evaluate the validity of the competing claims to the contested islands‘ sovereignty. Nor have we made an effort to do so to examine the legal concerns within the larger framework of the geopolitical situation.

This article is discussed in the following order. First, importance of disputes in South China Sea are summarized. Second, the prospects of China's approach towards the dispute are mentioned. Third, the relations between claimants are briefed. Fourth, describes how non-regional players can add new dimensions in solving dispute and finally, what should be India's approach towards the ASEAN and extra players.

Introduction

China's approach to Southeast Asia and its multiple territorial and maritime conflicts from the late 1990s until only a few years ago was to adopt a "good neighbour policy" and participate in bilateral discussions. This demonstrated Beijing's consideration for the opinions of others are concerned about China's ascent and the "China Threat." As a result, Beijing endeavored to be amicable and stick to Deng Xiaoping's past advice to defer territorial disputes for future generations while pursuing shared growth. Recently, though, Beijing's oil exploration and military operations in the South China Sea have grown more "assertive." Concerns about China's 'increasing assertiveness‘ and the 'China Threat‘ have prompted some ASEAN nations to deliberately invite the involvement of other major powers in the region, in particular to welcome renewed American efforts to reinvigorate bilateral security ties with Japan, the Philippines, Indonesia, and Vietnam. Together with Indian and Japanese engagement, this has led in the South China Sea being a focal point for great power competition, therefore exacerbating the situation. Despite the fact that the majority of competitor claimants are ASEAN member nations, China has historically attempted to handle the matter individually with each of the challenger's claims, not wanting it to become an issue in the primarily economic China-ASEAN relationship.

Extra-regional nations like as India and the United States have a vested interest in preserving the SCS, an environment that is home to a wealth of biodiversity and mineral wealth, including an estimated 190 quadrillion cubic feet of hydrocarbons. About 11 billion barrels of oil in proven and probable reserves, the majority of which are along the edges of the South China Sea as opposed to beneath disputed islands and reefs; much more yet to be found.

The Quest

The South China Sea is a semi-enclosed maritime region that is vital to international commerce and abundant in natural resources. Furthermore, it has regional and international economic importance. Nearly one-third of global trade and around fifty percent of global oil and gas exports transit via the sea yearly. 14 About $3.4 trillion worth of commodities pass through the Sea's waterways, comprising 14% of all U.S. commerce, 40% of China's, and 86% of Vietnam's.

The Sea also supplies around 12 percent of the world's seafood harvest, giving vital food safety and livelihoods to coastal residents in neighboring states. In recent years, territorial conflicts have been exacerbated by dwindling fish populations due to overfishing and decreased biodiversity. Regional tensions have also been heightened by disputes over seabed rights and drilling potential.

The South China Sea has considerable oil and gas deposits. In 2010, the U.S. Geological Survey estimated that 23 southeast Asian provinces bordering the Sea had an average of 21.6 billion untapped barrels of oil and approximately 300 trillion cubic feet of natural gas. Even more optimistically, Chinese assessments estimate up to 105 billion barrels of oil in the Spratly Islands continental shelf solely. Numerous businesses vie to harness these natural resources.

Ownership and Claims

The major legal argument in the South China Sea concerns whether state has the greater right to sovereignty over the contested outlying islands. The LOSC has no mechanisms for determining rival sovereignty claims islands or other geological features.

Claims of Sovereignty to Offshore Geographical Features

The norms and principles of international customary law governing the possession and territorial loss regulate this issue. The LOSC offers a comprehensive framework for international rule of the sea concerns. The LOSC defines the freedoms, rights, and duties of nations on the high seas and in the different maritime zones defined from terrestrial territories and islands. This is of special significance to the current topic. The LOSC presume that sovereignty has been established over the land territories and islands. Consequently, the LOSC is useless in settling territorial sovereignty conflicts in the South China Sea. Determining whether coastal State (or States) has (or have) sovereign rights over the contested islands of the South China Water is, nevertheless, immediately important to claim to maritime jurisdiction, in accordance with the time-honored legal principle that "the land trumps the sea."

Maritime claim for mainland terrtiory

All states surrounding the South China Sea assert an exclusive economic zone (EEZ) calculated from the baselines of their respective mainland coastlines or, in the case of Manila and Jakarta, from archipelagic baselines. The archipelagic baselines adopted by Indonesia and the Philippines surrounding their primary archipelago are congruent with the LOSC, as is commonly accepted.

Despite the fact that some straight baselines used across China, Malaysia, Taiwan, and Vietnam may be of dubious legality and may have a serious influence on the areas susceptible to the regimes of maritime boundary and territorial sea, they will have only a significant effect on the outer limit of the 200-nautical-mile exclusive economic zone (EEZ) claims evaluated from those baselines. For instance, the islands that Vietnam's straight baselines connect might establish their own maritime claims. This implies that the extension of the possible breadth of Vietnam's Economic zone is much more constrained than would otherwise be expected.

Spartly and Parcel Island

None of the ASEAN members have stated whether they claim an EEZ from any of the Spratly Islands about which they assert sovereignty. This is hardly unexpected, given it is arguably in their mutual benefit to sustain that every single island in the Spratlys are rocks as defined by Article 121(3) and have no right to their own EEZ and continental shelf. This would limit the "areas in conflicts" in the region surrounding the Spratly Islands to the 12-nautical-mile belt of territorial sea surrounding those features that meet the definition of an island, i.e., the naturally formed areas of land enveloped by and above water at high tide. This would be good for the ASEAN claimants since it would allow them to conduct marine resource development operations in South China Sea offshore regions close to their shores.

It seems, based on China's Notes Verbales dated 7 May 2009 and 11 April 2011, that China makes two distinct maritime space claims in the South China Sea.

First, it asserts 'sovereignty' over the islands (and maybe other geographical features) in the four archipelagos of the South China Sea, as well as the 'waters' around them. Near to the islands' probably refers to the 12-nautical-mile territorial waters adjoining to the islands.

Second, it asserts "sovereign rights and jurisdiction" over the "relevant waterways" and their seabeds and subsoils.

Exclusive economic zone and unclos

The UNCLOS creates a framework for maritime regulation in all oceans and seas, including the contentious South China Sea. The 1994 Convention, which replaced the 1958 "Convention on the High Seas," was signed and approved by the European Union and 167 other nations. UNCLOS also established a number of fundamental maritime organizations, including as the International Tribunal for the Law of the Sea (ITLOS), the International

Seabed Authority (ISA), and the Commission on the Limits of the Continental Shelf (CLCS).

The South China Sea features that fulfil the definition of an island in Article 121(1) are entitled, in theory, to their own EEZ and continental shelf. However, Article 121(3) states that they are not authorized to an EEZ and continental shelf if they are rocks incapable of supporting human occupancy or economic life. An island is immediately entitled to a continental shelf if it is not a rock only within definition of Article 121(3) If a State seeks to assert EEZ territory from an island or other land territory, it is required to file a legal claim. Practically speaking, the easiest choice for a Claimant would be to claim an EEZ from an island, since this would provide it sovereign powers to explore and utilize the natural riches of the seabed, subsoil, and adjacent waterways.

For instance, Beijing claims an EEZ from the Paracel Islands under its national law, but it has not specified the outside boundaries of its EEZ claim. China has asserted that the Spratly Islands are entitled to an EEZ and continental shelf, but it has not specified the metrics from which its maritime zones are calculated or the outer boundary of its EEZ or continental shelf entitlement in the Spratlys.

China's unilateral claims

HISTORICAL CLAIM: After Beijing submitted its nine-dashed line map to its Note Verbale to the UN Secretary-General dated May 6, 2009, doubts emerged over the importance of the map in relation to China's territorial claims in the South China Sea. The Verbal Note says stating "China has undisputed jurisdiction over the islands in the South China Sea and the surrounding seas, as well as sovereign rights and authority over the relevant waterways."

The dispute arises as to whether China claims rights and jurisdiction solely in the EEZ calculated from the archipelagos or in all seas inside the nine-dash line. Regarding jurisdiction, several Chinese national laws say that they apply not only in not just in China's maritime zones, perhaps also in all other marine regions under PRC administration. Some analysts have stated that "other sea regions under the sovereignty of the PRC" might apply to all coastal regions inside the nine-dash line. China also claims historic rights to the minerals located inside the nine-dash line.

Article 14 is the sole mention of historic rights in any official document of China's national law on the EEZ, which specifies that "the provisions of this Act must not impact the inherent jurisdiction of the People's Republic of China." However, this Act does not specify where China may have historical rights.

ASEAN VERSUS CHINA: As stipulated in Article 75 of the LOSC, none of the states surrounding the South China Sea have released official maps or catalogues of geographic coordinates depicting the outer boundary lines of their EEZ claims. Nonetheless, the boundaries of the Malaysian and Vietnamese EEZ claims are shown on maps included in their representations to the Commission on the Limits of the Continental Shelf.

Brunei, China, the Philippines, and Taiwan have not produced charts or coordinates demonstrating the outside boundary of their respective EEZ claims. It is intriguing that Malaysia and Vietnam's joint submission indicates a 200-nm EEZ boundary for the Philippines.

Several countries bordering the South China Sea are near to one another, necessitating the need for agreements to define their contiguous EEZ limits. Brunei and Malaysia seem to have addressed their nearby borders via a letter exchange, while China and Vietnam have struck a partial boundary deal in the Gulf of Tonkin.

In addition, Indonesia has delineated its continental shelf borders in the south-western region of the South China Sea with Malaysia and Vietnam. " Due to the Philippines' ancient sovereignty claim over the Malaysian state of Sabah, the border between Malaysia and the Philippines is a particularly sensitive issue.

If Brunei, China, and the Philippines increase their continental shelf claims in the South China Sea, the claims of Malaysia and Vietnam are likely to overlap. Moreover, Kuala Lumpur and Hanoi are probable to oppose their claims. Regardless of whether no maritime zones (like the EEZ and continental shelf) are claimed from the contested offshore islands, there will be substantial regions of overlapping continental shelf claims in the South China Sea between opposing States and nearby States.

New Maritime Law 2021:

MARITIME POLICE LAW (MPL): The Standing Committee of the National People's Congress of China passed a new Maritime Police Law (MPL) in January 2021 to oversee Chinese maritime agencies, including the Chinese Coast Guard. The law encompasses a wide variety of marine activities and interests, including measures to prohibit offshore smuggling, regulate fisheries, develop mineral wealth, safeguard the environment, and preserve maritime security. However, the law's ambiguous phrasing and expansive reach make it susceptible to misuse.

Example: 1. Article 3 specifies that enforcement agencies must undertake operations in Chinese waters, which probably covers unsettled seas claimed by China inside the nine-dash line.

73 UNCLOS limits the marine authority of a sovereign state to 12 nautical miles. Beyond these territorial waters, the law of the vessel's flag state governs. China claims sweeping authority over contested exclusive economic zones (EEZ) and waters along the continental shelf by using imprecise legislative terminology not recognized by UNCLOS, such as "waters subject to jurisdiction" or "jurisdictional seas." China's usage of unrecognized maritime borders is in violation of the PCA judgement and UNCLOS Article 74.

Example 2: Additionally, the MPL expands the use of force against foreign government boats and warships. Article 1, for instance, instructs China's Coast Guard and marine police to "defend the sovereignty of the State and preserve the fundamental interests of the people, companies, and other entities."

Example 3: Article 22 may permit military aggression, such as shooting against or ramming vessels, in response to foreign acts protected by freedom of navigation norms and UNCLOS laws. In addition, the MPL endangers the principles of freedom of navigation by empowering coastal police to limit or prevent passage based on the formation of interim maritime security zones.

THE MARITIME TRAFFIC SAFETY LAW:

China updated its 1983 Maritime Traffic Safety Law (MTSL) in April 2021 without consideration for international legal duties under UNCLOS. The geographic breadth of the amended regulation is contradictory with international law and appropriates illegal surveillance and interference with marine boats beyond of China's territorial waters. UNCLOS is violated by China's wide jurisdiction under the MTSL.

Example 1: Article 2, for instance, expands the scope of the new legislation from "coastal waters" to "sea regions under People's Republic of China authority."

Additionally, the MTSL permits illegal interference with foreign boats in breach of recognized freedom of navigation standards Article 19, for instance, allows China's Maritime Administrative Agency to impose ship restrictions.

Example 2: Article 43 similarly establishes a legal grey area that demands further compliance from boats operating in important fisheries or on regularly used shipping routes. In these places, captains may be required to increase their lookouts, slow down, or adhere to other Chinese navigational regulations. Routes and regulate marine traffic in extra-coastal seas.

As with previous law relationships, the ambiguity and overbreadth of these new laws provide Beijing with options to avoid and reinterpret its international legal duties under UNCLOS.

SOUTH ASIAN NATIONS AND ASEAN:

PHILIPPINES VERSUS CHINA ARBITRATION: In the Eritrea/Yemen Arbitration validates the position that traditional fishing rights of a third State in seas within the authority of a coastal State were not intrinsically destroyed by the LOSC and remain regulated by customary international law.

The Arbitral Tribunal in the Philippines v. China case will determine whether it has jurisdiction to hear the case, despite China's declaration under Article 298 excluding disputes involving the interpretation or application of Articles 15, 74, and 83 of the LOSC pertaining to sea boundary delimitations, as well as disputes involving historic bays or titles.

China's claims to historic rights through its nine-dash line were deemed invalid by the PCA.

China violated the Philippines' sovereign rights by intruding with fishing and resource research, and by aggravating other issues via the creation of artificial islands, according to the verdict. Ultimately, the PCA defined the features of "islands," ultimately removing China's contention that its manufactured islands produce legal claims under UNCLOS. The court ruled that elements of the Spratly Islands did not justify China's territorial claim. Nevertheless, the PCA recognized that it lacks the ability to determine territorial sovereign borders or marine delimitation.

VIETNAM, CHINA AND SOUTH CHINA SEA:

Lack of consensus over the extent of South China Sea conflicts is a serious concern between the nations. On the agenda is just the issue about the Spratly archipelago. China is opposed to any mention of the Paracel Islands. Vietnam China rejects the inclusion of regions east of the Vietnamese coast where Vietnam's claims to the continental shelf and EEZ reach inside the boundary of China's so-called nine dashed lines. If China and Vietnam could reach a consensus on the breadth and contentious topics, it would be a significant step toward establishing an agenda for expert-level discussions that would also contribute to international efforts. This does not imply that either party should forsake their sovereignty claims; rather, they should acknowledge that their rights overlap and that the situation requires attention. Even if they deem the other party's claims to be invalid, the two parties should admit that the other party has claims.

China and Vietnam may contribute favorably to the prosperity of the area. The implementation of the 2002 DOC and the process of building the conflict management tools required to preserve peace and avert tension in the South China Sea, such as a South China Sea-applicable regional code of conduct.

THE QUAD NATIONS:

Since its resurrection in 2017, the Quad has restated its commitment to a free and open Indo-Pacific. On 13 July 2020, the then-Secretary of State of the United States, Mike Pompeo, issued a statement reflecting the stiffening of US policy in a "important, contested section of the Indo-Pacific region, the South China Sea." The statement claimed, "Beijing's China's claims to living marine resources in the majority of the South China Sea are illegal, as is its campaign of intimidation to control them. In 2016, the Permanent Court of Arbitration at The Hague ruled in favor of the Philippines, declaring that China's historical claims to the marine resources were "illegal" and not covered by the UNCLOS.

In November 2020, Tokyo and Canberra reached an agreement on a groundbreaking defense deal permitting reciprocal visits for exercises and operations, and expressed worry about the contested SCS. The agreement permits Japanese and Australian forces to visit one another's territory.

Japan's Prime Minister Yoshihide Suga and his Australian counterpart Scott Morrison, who was visiting Tokyo at the time, reached an agreement in principle to undertake training and cooperative operations in each other's nations..

ASEAN nations, particularly Vietnam, welcomed India as an outsider participant. The Indian navy warship INS Airavat docked to Nha on July 22, 2011.A Chinese notice advised Trang in southern Vietnam to stay away of Chinese seas. The Indian Foreign Ministry said, "India upholds freedom of navigation in international waterways, including the South China Sea, and the right of passage in conformity with internationally recognized legal norms." In the meanwhile, China has opposed the exploratory operations of India's Oil and Natural Gas Corp (ONGC) in the Paracel Islands (claimed by Vietnam), a sensitive issue for China. ONGC is of the opinion that Vietnamese claims are consistent with international law, and it will proceed with exploratory operations in two blocks close to the Paracel Islands.

The central Japanese concept was a multilateral strategy, including Japan and ASEAN's other discussion partners, to establish a maritime regime in the South China Sea. South China Sea on the basis of freedom of navigation, international law, and peaceful conflict resolution.

Thus, Indian and Japanese engagement in the region and their burgeoning connections with the Philippines and Vietnam exacerbate the situation in the South China Sea and increase the likelihood that one of the parties may miscalculate. India views Southeast Asia as the pivot linking the Indian and Pacific Oceans, hence reinforcing the Indo-Pacific strategy ideas.

1- India is completely dedicated to a free and open Indo-Pacific region and to upholding an international order based on norms. It is often the first person to respond in any Humanitarian Assistance and Disaster Relief (HADR) mission, and it actively participates in several regional security conferences.

2- Effective maritime enforcement capability starts with strong marine domain awareness (MDA), which is defined as the capacity to collect, process, analyze, and communicate real-time information about what is happening at sea.

3- India has previously partnered with Vietnam and the Philippines on capacity-building efforts. India and Vietnam elevated their relationship to a "comprehensive strategic partnership" in 2016. Both parties have reached an agreement to share white shipping data. Additionally, India is considering supplying warships to the Vietnamese Coast Guard.

4- India has investigated overseas markets outside of Southeast Asia to supply the Brahmos missile system. India should now contemplate exporting Brahmos missiles to nations such as the Philippines and Indonesia.

5- India and the other Quad partners are permitted to enter. India can encourage the United States, Japan, and Australia to engage in Southeast Asian infrastructure development and, by extension, the ASEAN Masterplan on Connectivity 2025.

6- Extra-regional actors such as India, the United States, Japan, and Australia may continually emphasise the need for China to respect international law in the South China Sea (SCS) and for a speedier completion of the COC on terms acceptable to both China and the claimant ASEAN states.

This may assist in exerting stress on the Chinese government on a variety of international venues.

Conclusion

Some ASEAN nations continue to have doubts over China's long-term objectives in Southeast Asia, despite China's growing status as a political and economic force in the region. This uncertainty, their growing nationalist sentiment at home, and their persistent exploration for oil and gas throughout the South China Sea will continue to stir up conflict within their already fraught bilateral ties with China.

Since the end of the Cultural Revolution, China's national confidence has soared to new heights thanks to the country's rapid economic development. The United States is reasserting its presence in the Asia-Pacific region and putting forth an effort to strengthen its ties with the Philippines and Vietnam. At the same time, Chinese nationalists are increasingly blaming the government for what they perceive to be a lack of action and are pressing for a more forceful stance. The participation of New Delhi and Tokyo has also contributed to an increase in the intensity of the situation. It is to be anticipated that the growing bellicosity of recent pronouncements does not portend a scenario that is either more difficult on the land or on the sea. It seems that Chinese President and the Communist Party are becoming more eager to use the legal system to bolster the legitimacy of the administration. It is very necessary for those working in international law to recognise the dangers of authoritarian tendencies in the field and take steps to counteract them. In regard to the disagreements that have arisen in the South China Sea, I have a few proposals. A legally-binding code of behavior for coastal nations offers the promise of stability and has the potential to benefit all parties involved in the claim. Enhancing UNCLOS's ability to enforce its provisions is another strategy that may be used to promote state compliance. There is a lot more that can be done, both by individual nations and by international organizations, to advance multilateralism in maritime governance. The failure to properly control and safeguard the world's seas and oceans will have devastating effects on coastal populations as well as marine ecosystems if it is allowed to continue. A next generation of international accords that will safeguard biodiversity outside national authorities and create a genuine system for oceanic responsibility is long overdue. These agreements have been in the works for far too long.

CHAPTER XVIII

Consensual sexual intercourse between same-sex people is an "unnatural offence"

Written by Vansh Dhingra (4th Semester, BA. LL.B - Chandigarh University, Mohali).

Introduction

Before we proceed the article, we need to ensure we comprehend what do we truly mean when we utilize the expression "Unnatural Sexual Offense "and how could it be not quite the same as assault. A few regulations were made to depict Assault and its disciplines and a few regulations were made to portray Unnatural sexual offense and its disciplines. In this way we should discuss Assault, right off the bat. "Assault" emerges from the Latin word 'rapio' which means to seize.

Assault is a sexual infringement against the desire of a ladies, by extortion or power. Section 375 of The Indian Correctional Code manages sections connected with assault and its discipline. Section 377 of the IPC condemns any "unnatural" offenses with either life detainment or detainment which might reach out to a decade, and a fine. It draws lined up from regulations restricting homosexuality and savagery in Britain. It is vital to take note of that assent is completely irrelevant with regards to unnatural sexual offenses.

Presently, The Dark's regulation word reference characterizes normal as a something unadulterated or genuine recognized from something counterfeit or invented and to figure out what regular means is that each instrument or organ of the body had a particular capability to perform, and consequently, involving such an organ for a specific reason against its chief capability is unnatural According to this rationale, each type of sex other than penile vaginal will be viewed as unnatural.

Likewise, something besides procreative sex as unnatural. This rationale however by all appearances counter-intuitive has been supported by courts in different cases. In Khanu v Head it was held that "the regular object of animalistic intercourse is that there ought to be the chance of origination of people, which on account of copulation per os is unimaginable

I. The (unnaturally) natural homosexual

Examining into the bunch manners by which the judgment revives the hetero legend involves an outline of the judgment in any event, when the disintegration of the legend is planned. The judgment which has beenthe reason for much festival holds that "Section 377 IPC, to the extent that it condemns consensual sexual demonstrations of grown-ups in private, is violative of Articles 21, 14 and 15 of the Constitution."15 The closing sections embracing the subject of comprehensiveness of the Constitution of India affirm that "those apparent by the larger part as 'degenerates' or 'different' are not on that score prohibited or alienated" and that misinterpretations about who the LGBTs16 (lesbian, gay, sexually open and transsexual) are, ought to not illuminate regulation. The remainder of the archive is obviously how the court shows up at this 'notable' judgment. Section 377 was conceived out of a longing to physically teach the provincial subject envisioned as suggestively unreasonable in 1860. It condemns "unnatural offenses" which incorporate intentional "licentious intercourse" against the "request for nature" with any man, lady or then again creature Section 377 further elucidates that infiltration is adequate to cause 'lustful intercourse'. 'Lustful intercourse' in this case, has been deciphered as butt-centric sex, oral sex and different types of non-procreative albeit penetrative sexual acts.

Curiously, the law doesn't separate between 'gay people' furthermore 'heteros'; both stand ensnared and possibly blamable of conflicting with nature. Kindly note that the words 'gay' and 'hetero' were at this point to be developed when the law was drafted by Master Macaulay and, since their development, have not been consolidated in the law. Section 377, then, in fact addresses the picture of the homosexual alone. The homosexual is a man with an unpredictable profound quality furthermore, distorted sexual preferences; at any rate, by Christian principles (all salvation religions censure homosexuality, to be exact). Albeit the homosexual turns into a gay in the end, conflating a homosexual with a gay would be a desultory sin. A homosexual enjoys sexual acts that welcome strict judgment and lawful banishment while a 'gay' is an individual with a variant sexual personality. Homosexuality indicates demonstrations of offense while the gay is comprised with an intrusive subjectivity.

The subjectivity of the homosexual, notwithstanding, stays more tricky and curiously nonexclusive; conventional as in it suggests a corrupt unreasonable 'sinister' demeanor which can unleash ruin on any psyche (the minds are yet to be heterosexualised/homosexualised). This enemy of homosexuality regulation establishes specific stable conditions. The regular isn't criminal. It can't be so for the regular additionally seems, by all accounts, to be compulsory (a decree of the divine maybe). The unnatural is a demonstration of volition subsequently the homosexual decides to sin; sin isn't yet his comprising quintessence.

The homosexual is a simple burst, a flashing crack as a physically prohibited act in the generally regular world and naturalized being. Nature, in this case, can be reestablished. The homosexual can be changed over completely to his normally moral self (ostensibly through corrective measures). One must always remember that the normal is likewise consistently upright and one must likewise take cognisance of the way that the moral is comprised as ahistorical. So the law places into place the effortlessness of copulation between a man and a lady.

Bodily intercourse between a man's penis and a lady's vagina is normal to the point that it didn't need a demonstration of naming. Homosexuality then worked to name not just a longing that dare not tell its name yet additionally to discuss a longing so regular, moral and clear that it shouldn't need to have a name by any stretch of the imagination. Homosexuality is appropriated to represent the normal craving. While the previous was an 'loosely held bit of information, the last option was an unbiased, all inclusive, strict truth. 1869 is the year while restricting twins are conveyed to information - 'gay' and 'hetero', with a view to highlight a particular shift that had been occurring in Europe with respect to comprehension of sexuality.

Sexuality started to work not through a math of recommended furthermore, banished sexual demonstrations yet through an order of people and characters. Sexuality turned into a science. Furthermore, that's what science affirmed the gay people are a divisible animal categories through and through; not an impermanent deviation yet a normally happening inconsistency and until the late 20th century, clinical/mental science was undaunted in its reparative position of fixing this anomaly.18 The confidence that nature could be reestablished stayed in salvageable shape. It had another name: heterosexuality. Some more steady conditions follow:

Hetero = normal and Gay = unnatural (be that as it may, all the while normally happening);

Regular = ordinary and unusual = unnatural.

II. The homosexual erasure from the public and the private

Section 377 has been only here and there applied in court judgements19 however its very presence has pushed guiltiness on same-sex wanting people driving them 'underground', covering them under the building of a country that prohibits them and hinders their capacity to profit open doors toward an honorable life. One should shun proposing an outright causal connection between Section 377 and homophobia in India, yet the law gives a fertile site for the explanation of homophobia and reactions against it. It delivers any type of strange distinguishing proof in every case currently freak.

As anyone might expect, then, at that point, the twenty years old strange development in India has to a great extent been a battle against Section 377. In 1994, ABVA (Helps Bhedbhav Virodhi Andolan) a left-wing, non-subsidized bunch documented a request against Section 377 in the Delhi High Court scrutinizing its established legitimacy. The request was documented at the command of a clinical report which affirmed that Tihar Prison had turned into a homosexual's sanctuary.

WHO (World Health Organization) had suggested conveyance of condoms to the detainees. Expecting that it would add fuel to fire (or want) also, advance what the law as of now disallows, prison specialists rejected. The case came in the mood for hearing in 2001 and was excused without the information on ABVA, which had neglected to monitor it.

Conclusion

The state can't belittle their reality or control their fate by making their confidential sexual direct a crime. The Indian courts need to perceive that they can't allow the state to keep on disparaging the presence of individuals with same sex wants in this country. S 377 with its more extensive shadow of culpability is the greatest attack against the pride and humankind of a significant minority of Indian residents. The courts need to recognize that by decriminalizing homosexuality they won't allow a simple sexual action, yet decriminalize the existences of real residents who are associated with that sexual demonstration.

CHAPTER XIX

Adultery: Apple of Discord

Written by Juli Rai (4th Semester, BA. LL.B - Chandigarh University, Mohali).

Introduction

Whoever has sex with an individual who is and whom he knows or has the motivation to accept to be the spouse of another man, without the assent or intrigue of that man, such sex not adding up to the offense of rape, is at fault for the offense of infidelity, and will be rebuffed with the detainment of one or the other depiction for a term which might stretch out to five years, or with fine, or with both. In such case the spouse will not be culpable as an abettor.

Law adultery in India

As opposed to the country's inappropriate behaviour rules, which depend on ladies' collaboration, the 158-year-old infidelity regulation neglected to regard ladies' will. Indeed in the event that the spouse agreed to the lead, ladies can't be rebuffed under the law, yet a spouse can sue a man who has intercourse with his significant other. On the off chance that, then again, a spouse has an undertaking, neither he nor his significant other can be sought after. As it converged with an individual, Indian infidelity regulation assumed the pride of ladies. The demonstration rebuffed a male who was thought of engaging in extramarital relations with a wedded lady, yet it didn't make a difference to ladies. Ladies have seldom been rebuffed for infidelity since they are viewed as blameless casualties. In the viewpoint of the law, she had no singular life and was viewed as her significant other's property. The regulation has been upheld by the way that marriage is a blessed body that was purportedly disregarded by a blessed man, and in this way exclusively by the individual who was culpable.

Afterward, during the procedures testing the lawfulness of Section 497 of the IPC, Dipak Misra, then-Leader of the High Court of India, expressed, "It is up to the couple worried to safeguard wedded couples." Assuming one fizzles, the other is allowed a legitimate cure (separate from regulation). In a bombed marriage, where is the "public great" question?

The High Court announced in 1985 that "the tempter is typically the male, not the lady," and that orientation killing the regulation would consider "a ladies on-a woman cruise." This section (section 497 of the Indian Punitive Code, 1860) framed results that could incorporate a five-year jail sentence, a punishment, or both. This state doesn't punish the spouse regardless of whether she is an abettor.

As indicated by the Code of Criminal System, a double-crossing spouse isn't qualified for support. A help request might be repealed in the event that evidence of her living in infidelity is given. Be that as it may, living in infidelity isn't equivalent to committing infidelity once.

"Captivating your significant other away from you to commit infidelity with her is culpable under sections 498 and 497 of the Indian Reformatory Code. Section 497 of the Indian Correctional Code 1860 contains the accompanying key fixings." An individual high priority sex with another man's significant other; the individual should be aware or have motivation to accept that the lady is another man's significant other; the spouse didn't give sexual movement endorsement or conspiracy; furthermore, this kind of sex isn't a rape offense.

Infidelity isn't cleared by a lady's understanding or solicitation. No court will be made mindful of the offense (infidelity) under Section 198 of the 1973 Code of Criminal Strategy except if a lady's better half or, without even a trace of the spouse, someone else who really focused on the spouse in the interest of the husband whined with the court's approval assuming an infidelity was committed at that point.

Decriminalizing Adultery

In December 2017, Joseph Sparkle, a 41-year-old Indian money manager living in Italy, recorded a Public Interest Prosecution with the High Court of India, requesting the annulment of the adultery regulation. Contrasting section 497 with section 198 of the Indian Reformatory Code, he accepted it abused Articles 14, 15, and 21 since it exclusively considered guys responsible for extramarital issues and regarded ladies as articles. This began as a bogus PIL. The applicant guarantees the condition condemns adultery exclusively founded on sex classification. Spouse assent is unessential. Thus, it breaks Article 14. A woman is her better half's property, as indicated by him. Adultery isn't committed when the spouse assents or schemes. The candidate asserts the provision is unlawful in light of the fact that it breaks Article 21 by slighting a lady's poise and sexual independence. In October 2017, José Shine, a non-occupant Keralite, sent off a public interest suit in Joseph Shine v. Union of India. Adultery was charged under Section 497 of the Indian Punitive Code (1860) and Section 198(2) of the Code of Criminal Strategy (1973). Section 497 of the Indian Penal Code of 1860 rebuffs adultery by requiring the spouse's assent or information. For an offense under sections 497 and 498 of the Indian Penal Code of 1860, a complainant may present a charge under section 198(2) of the Criminal Method Code.

The issues include:

1. Does the adultery condition in Article 14 segregate?
2. Is it genuine that the adultery arrangement encourages the possibility that ladies are male property and abuses Article 15 by sex segregation?
3. Is it disparaging to a lady's poise to deny her sexual independence and independence?
4. Is it genuine that rebuffing adultery is a legitimate intrusion of an individual's protection?

Adultery as a ground for divorce

Adultery is a legitimate reason for petitioning for legal separation in the event that one of the accomplices commits it. Adultery happens when an individual has sexual relations with the companion of another. This happens at the point when people who are not hitched participate in sexual movement. Since it is consensual, it very well may be considered treachery or an extramarital undertaking. Profound quality is basic in marriage, which is the reason both a couple should be devoted. When one accomplice engages in extramarital relations, the other accomplice becomes untrustworthy to their life partner. Divorce is a troublesome process; hence, prior to recording, think about the repercussions of life after divorce. In India, divorce is as yet slandered by the person's family, with the ramifications that a woman divorced by her better half has a less lucky existence than her companion. In India, the greater part of ladies can't help monetarily. In the event that the couple had youngsters, the youngsters would experience the most. Assuming that one grown-up accomplice defies the other before the youngsters, absolution is ideal than case.

CHAPTER XX

Juvenile Justice System: Treatment and Interventions

Written by Shristhi Singh (2nd Semester, BA. LL.B - Chandigarh University, Mohali).

Abstract

The way to cut the roots of the problem of transgressions of law is to make sure the populace does not deviate into such matters from an early age, this article presents an insight on juvenile delinquency and a thorough view is presented on the patterns of delinquency throughout history amongst distinct societies, their views and attempts at controlling juvenile Delinquency, this article continues to examine the various causes that play a major role in the development of deviant behaviour

Introduction

Adolphus Quetlet, who was a Belgian, statistician quoted "the propensity to crime is at its maximum at the age when strength and passions have reached their height, yet when reason has not acquired sufficient control to master their combined influence." A child when born is always innocent, it depends upon the circumstances and surroundings on how the person turns out to be. When a child is fed with tender care and attention, fulfillment of their needs are done, they bloom to be socially, mentally, physically and ethically moral citizens of they society on the other hand absence of these major aspectual needs may result in the child being delinquent.

Delinquency can be defined as the impulsiveness in adolescents that leads them to commit any kind of crime. The age of the delinquents lie between 15-18. Delinquency is the behavior that doesn't comply with the legal and moral aspects of the society. The word 'delinquency' has been sourced from Latin word "delinquer" which meant 'to omit'. Initially it was used by Romans to refer to a person who had failed to perform certain task or duty that were assigned to them. The term delinquent was first used by William Coxson in the year 1484 to denote a person found guilty of customary offence.

In simple words Delinquency is misbehavior or variance from the normally accepted norms in the society in terms of conduct. Special treatment for the juvenile offenders started to take place around the end of eighteenth century.

Precedent to this juvenile offenders were dealt in the same way as that of adult offenders. the sentence served by them was also with the adults in the same prison. This acted as breeding ground for villainy and criminality. The juveniles got associated with the criminals an greater evil of society and after completing their sentence and coming into society they would implement the learnings and cause impairment.

In India, provisions like furnishing with care, treatment, protection and help in development and rehabilitation of the derelicts or the juveniles. Their trial is enacted under Juvenile Justice (Care and Protection of Children) Act 2000. The exact definition of juvenile delinquency still is open to debate and is mostly made on personal interpretations of an individual. On Prevention of Crime and Treatment of offenders the Second United Nations congress engaged in problem of juvenile delinquency and unanimously the decision was taken that the problem of definition need not be stretched any further and its meaning in terms of its label be limited to its breach of criminal law and ill-adjusted etiquettes that are looked down upon by the society.

First Instances of Juvenile Delinquency

Envisaging the time during the 1600-1800s when a committing a crime at age 13 and being bound in a space with adult wrongdoer or having to suffer the jarring and barbarous punishment. On going Juvenile Justice System makes it certain and guarantees that the juveniles are allocated the resources properly and to rehabilitate the juveniles by reaching out to them at their homes and through factions of the society.

Preceding to the 1800s if a crime was committed by an adolescent they were punished in the way same to as the adults. The dogma of serving and handling the delinquents same as to the adults was emanated from English Common Law. Some practices that were followed under the English Common Law were- the juveniles were obligated to work and train for agricultural and domiciliary work and for some to contract with adulthood. All these practices swiftly aided itself into America and fireballed till the early 19th century. The same practices were being followed and the juvenile delinquents were being tested and penalized as adults for the crimes committed by them. The diplomatic leaders resolved to fixate and find substitutive ways attenuate the difficult circumstances which the juveniles were condemned to. The objective was to come up with newly made schemes, projects and campaigns to dispense guidance and protection to the youth.

19th century was the dawn of child saving movement with the main area of focus being able to construct and manufacture schemes engaged on correcting the behaviour of the juveniles. To execute this goal New York House of Refuge was instated in 1825. The delinquents who were on the verge to end up on the street were taken up through this to refine them into a surrounding that would be advantageous to them.

Most of the adolescents who were taken in, into the House of Refuge were offender or childeren whose parents weren't able to look out for kids. The court commanded them to be admitted to this institution for them to be molded in a way that would be beneficial for them. The House of Refuge in a decennary of it's up and running had around 1600 juveniles who they were working with. Comprehending it's success many more institutions of similar kind were established. The downfall of these institutions were the treatment of the juveniles over the years as they deteriorated in the reception. There was excess of crowd of the juveniles, busted conditions and concern among the management.

Causes for Juvenile Delinquency:

Social Factors

Due to expansion and economic magnification India culminated in urbanization which contributed to stem more new problems like accomodations, blighted area, overpopulation, dearth of parental guidance and household dissolution and many more. The expensive ways of residing in urban areas required it's residents to practise outdoor jobs for the maintenance of their family whether it be male or female and the out-turn of this forsaken children without any parental guidance.

Economic Factor

The inclination towards present day splendour entices the youngsters to turn towards unreasonable means to appease their desires. Living in poverty far away from all the materialistic objects creates a longing for it. All these elements collectively steer towards the vast growth in the juvenile delinquency.

Biological Factors

Anatomical maturity, low intellect also results in delinquent behaviour . Genetic make up of a person is also responsible for this behaviour. Ecological and environmental framework also plays chief set off in the entity of the juvenile. A study shows that today Indian girls and boys attain puberty 3-4 years on an average, while mentally and psychologically they are naive and unable to formulate actuality of life. It's aspired that parents should elucidate the repercussions of certain unwanted and prohibited action to their children.

Abuse

Substance abuse is a crucial element in the mass of the juvenile delinquent cases. Presently the youth are utilizing high powered drugs as compared to adolescents a decade ago. They start using them earlier as well at a trivial age. Use of these drugs usher the adolescents to commit crimes by engrossing themselves pernicious, detrimental and illegitimate undertaking.

Family background

The extraordinary surge in divorce cases and matrimonial fall out is yet additional element that deranges familial accord. Upon feeling neglected a child is apprenticed to get adrift and this provides provision for juvenile delinquency. A child need safeguarding, endearment and direction at their home. Considerable significance should be paid to help them guide towards intercepting from entertaining criminal behaviour rather than correcting the committed misdemeanour.

Remedies and Treatment

The stratagem for course of action against juvenile delinquency under the Juvenile Justice Act, 2000 is different from ordinary criminal trial. It's termed as 'special procedure'. The following provisions have been granted and guaranteed by the Indian Constitution to particularly the children:

Article 21: A Right to free and compulsory education;

Article 24: Right to be protected from hazardous employment till 14 years of age;

Article 39(e): Right to be protected from being abused and forced by economic necessity to enter occupations unsuited to their age or strength;

Article 39(f): Right to equal opportunities and facilities to develop in a healthy manner and in conditions of freedom and dignity and guaranteed protection of childhood and youth against exploitation and against moral and material abandonment;

Article 45: Right to early childhood care and education to all children until they complete the age of 6 years.

Child Welfare Committees

These are independent bodies qualified to deal with children who are in desperate need of care and protection. Its necessary to have at least one welfare committee in every district to exert power and implement the duties. It includes a chairperson and four other members who can discharge those duties and are suitable according to the State government.

Shelter homes

It implies that State Government should acknowledge reputative and competent voluntary organization and provide them assistance to construct and administer as many shelter homes possible. For juveniles as much is required.

Rehabilitation and Social Re-integration

Rehabilitation and reintegration of a juvenile should start during the course of their stay in children home which should alternately be carried by i) adoption ii) foster care iii) sponsorship iv) after care organisation.

Conclusion

Through this paper, various aspects of the juvenile justice system are analyzed and presented with the motive to discuss the preventive measures and remedies prescribed to juvenile offenders by different societies in different points of time, and the different ailments for the such by said societies are compared and the difference in viewpoints are observed and discussed. It is important to mention these differences as it marks the philosophy of the time and the change in society is observed, that with development in the field of science and justice systems, the treatment of juvenile offenders has increased immensely, from being subjugated to the capital punishments in ancient times to being enrolled in programs that improve their conditions, this is the purpose of the enquiry that has been conducted through this paper, following this, the several factors which contribute to juvenile delinquency are discussed in detail to gather a complete perception of the issue at hand, monitoring and controlling the juvenile offense rates for the establishment of a crime free society.

Printed by Libri Plureos GmbH in Hamburg,
Germany